LAW
OF
LIFE

By A. D. K. LUK

Books by A. D. K. Luk

Law of Life Book I, & Book II
Life and Teaching of Jesus and Mary
Law of Life and Teachings by Divine Beings
Law of Life Songs
Group Outline and Decree Booklet
Group Activities Instruction Booklet
Law of Life for Children Booklet
Colored Chart

Published and Distributed by

A. D. K. Luk Publications

A.D.K. LUK Publication
P.O. Box 530035
St. Petersburg, FL 33747

BOOK II

DEDICATION

This book is dedicated to the Great Ones—the Divine Beings; may it serve as a connection with the outer consciousness of mankind and enlightenment to all interested. May it bring about an understanding and closer feeling toward Them and help bring about the conscious association once more of man with the Angels and Elemental kingdom.

PREFACE

This book is brought forth in response to many requests from students and others who are interested.

It was made possible under the guidance and direction of the Ascended Masters, Who have given this information concerning Themselves and Their Homes.

This instruction gives knowledge about the Ascended Masters and Their Plans, Their activities and Individual services, to mankind and the Earth at this time; also explains how to invoke and draw forth this assistance so much needed.

Book I and Book II were set up to be published together. Later it was decided that for practical reasons as well as for convenience sake, and the purpose the author wished to achieve would be better served if the subject matter was published separately.

The writing and compilation of this work (Book II) was completed in 1958.

CONTENTS

SHAMBALLA

Shamballa—built through the nine hundred years,
  In ethers, to inner sight now appears,
Tall minarets and cosmic rainbow hue,
  With atmosphere a great sea of sapphire blue.

A City pulsating above the Gobi sand,
  Connected by marble bridge to mainland.
Trees, terraces, fountains, Temple with golden dome
  For the "Lord of the World"—His Sacred Home.

To Shamballa, Sanat Kumara from Venus came
  With the other Kumaras—"Lords of the Flame",
Bringing to Earth new hope for redemption
  Through the Sacred Fire's action of purification.

Shamballa, where dwelt "The Ancient of Days"
  Whose Holy Presence changed mankind's ways.
All Messengers from Thy Sacred Halls have come
  With marvelous Truth in love, illumining some.

His voluntary exile from the planet Venus,
  Millions of years in sacrifice for us,
Until by our light His ransom we pay,
  With a place in this system permanently stay.

He, in His patience sustained the Earth
  Through the centuries until her new birth;
When through mankind enough light would expand,
  To become now a great radiating sun.

Shamballa—His Earthly Home, a paradise sublime,
  Shall again manifest physically a fourth time,
And be thus sustained throughout eternity,
  A perfect outpicturing of Divinity.

Shamballa, Holy City of King of Kings,
  To Whose feet each one his harvest brings,
Placing it on the Altar in His Name;
  Whereon stands visible, the great Three-fold Flame.

Now, when the close of the cycle has come,
  He returning to His Beloved and His Home;
Through His great Love all mankind did raise,
  To Him shall we forever give our great sincere praise.

CREATION

Two Cosmic Beings take the initiation to become Sun God and Sun Goddess and are endowed with the power to create a system of worlds. They then design within Their consciousness the plan of Their solar system, the number, type, size and formation of each planet with all the details; also the number and type of lifestreams to evolve or develop upon each planet.

They then draw to Themselves through cohesive power a Cosmic Silent Watcher Who offers to hold within His or Her own consciousness and Being the light pattern for the planets of the solar system. They also draw to Themselves the Elohim of Creation (there are seven for this system), Who offer to help build the planets, each in its appointed time. They draw the Builders of Form, Archangels, The Directors of the Four Elements, Devas, Seraphim, Cherubim, Angels; and Guardians also are drawn forth.

The creation of a planet takes place by the Sun God and Sun Goddess formulating a design which is given to a chosen Planetary Silent Watcher Who maintains the design in the consciousness.

The creation of a planet takes place by the cooperation of the Silent Watcher, the Seven Elohim, the Builders of Form, Devas, the Directors of the Four Elements and the beings of the elements.

The Seven Elohim build the form of the planets. They represent the mental activity or radiation. The Seven Archangels represent and supply the (spiritual) feeling activity or radiation.

The Seven Elohim get the design from the Planetary Silent Watcher. The Elohim (masculine and feminine) project forth Their combined light rays and where they meet or cross the permanent atom is formed—the Three-fold Flame, around which is drawn the electronic light substance, creating the planet. These two rays are the Two Permanent Rays to that planet.

In the center of the planet is the magnetizing focus, a similar action as the Three-fold Flame in the heart, that holds the atoms of the physical body together. This forms the cohesive power for the electrons or atoms of the earth, water and air elements.

There has to be a natural gravity—a magnetic pull for a planet to hold things and mankind to it; that is controlled by the Rod of Power which is kept at Shamballa. Along with this magnetic pull mankind have tied their energies with earth substance by human desires and appetites through the senses, which makes the heavy gravity pull of Earth; thus preventing levitation which should be a natural activity. It is the binding force.

There are Cosmic Beings Who offer Their service to formulate the axis, such as Polaris and Magnus, Who sustain the axis for the Earth at the present time.

Earth was created through the rhythmic release of the outpouring of the Seven Elohim over a long period of time until it reached a point of completeness, and the Three-fold Flame in the center began its function and the Earth began to revolve upon its axis. It is radiation from the Sun that causes a planet to rotate on its axis, and move in its orbit around the Sun.

When the elements have been drawn together then the light energy from the Sun (the fire element) inter-penetrates the planet, establishing the fecundating power of the fire element, and the various Cosmic Beings give Their specific elements—virtues which make the planet a habitable place for individualized Flames in physical form.

When the planet Earth was to be created, Virgo and Pelleur (Twin Rays) offered Their services to produce or supply the substance of the earth element, which would hold form for the water element as well as provide (stationary) substance, or substance of a vibratory rate that would support the weight of the bodies of mankind, and upon which they could live. This earth substance was created from the atoms formed by drawing (pure) electrons around a central core. The substance of Earth in the beginning was completely pure and of a more rapid vibratory rate than now, therefore not nearly so dense. It was similar to what we now know as the ethers. Other planets function at more rapid vibrations, on the original plan. The earth element was originally pure substance and the colors of the seven rays played through it producing an iridescent radiance. Pelleur's radiance from the center permeated the entire Earth.

The Directors of the Elements, Virgo, Neptune, Aries and Helios or a Director of the fire element, with Their beings of the elements, the Gods of the Mountains and of the Sea, Amaryllis (the Goddess of Spring) and the various Devas then created the mountains, rivers, valleys, mineral and plant life, trees, shrubs, flowers and all that goes to make up a beautiful planet. Gold and jewels were placed in the Earth to give out radiation. They grow similar to plant life through radiation from great Beings Who direct these activities.

All creation takes place to the rhythm of music.

The Sun God and Goddess in the meantime draw forth Individualizations to people the planet.

Each individual's life does not begin at birth of a physical body but with the projecting forth of a light ray from the hearts of the Sun God and Goddess; at the end of that ray a flame comes into being, a Three-fold Flame, around which coalesces light substance and the creation of the Divine Presence takes place, thus forming an individual God-Flame. The awareness of "I AM" by the Three-fold Flame makes It an *Individual* with free will. The God-Flame is then an Individual Creator—a co-Creator with God, the Cosmic I AM Presence.

These abide in the aura of the God-Parents for the time being. Some return and become un-individualized again. Those choosing to go on out further in the scheme of creation project forth two rays—Twin Rays, at the end of each a Three-fold Flame around which is drawn light substance, forming what is known as the

Electronic Body, wherein abides the "I AM" Who knows Itself as an Individual, which we term the I AM Presence. (See Twin Rays page 140.)

Then these Intelligences begin Their journey through the seven inner spheres, through which They must pass before They are ready to embody on a planet. They know primal life is Theirs to use. There They begin to create through the I AM Consciousness that which They see, in whatever sphere They abide. They learn to use Their thought and feeling centers, to create form by thought, then through joyous feeling to energize it. There They absorb the qualities of each sphere, remaining in each as long as desired, thus forming a Causal Body.

They are permitted to enjoy the various activities and qualities of each sphere, assimilate those qualities and through their own use of primal life, through thought and feeling build the quality and color of that sphere into their own Causal Bodies. They are taken into the first sphere and after a certain length of time those who wish to progress further are taken to the second sphere. Some however prefer to remain in the first sphere, likewise some choose to go on to the third and there are those who wish to remain in the second sphere, and so on through the seven spheres.

Those choosing to remain in the various spheres become the Brothers and Sisters of that particular sphere, forming a part of the Hosts of Heaven and rendering service at inner levels for eternity.

Those who progressed through the seven spheres in their development and wish to take embodiment can, under the direction and guidance of the Manu for a particular root race, take embodiment on a planet. Each one has a certain amount of development from each sphere which he has absorbed, according to interest, intensity and length of time spent there. This results in a varying of momentum, size and color of the sphere or band of the Causal Body, the predominant quality in the Causal Body denoting which ray he is on. This makes him primarily a being of that ray. He can then take physical embodiment on a planet under the direction of a Manu. These Beings are placed within the keeping of the Planetary Silent Watcher (a feminine Being), and They continue creation in the seven spheres until They are called forth to embody. The Manu (being of the masculine activity) draws forth a portion of these individualizations for His root race. The Causal Body of the Planetary Silent Watcher makes up the seven spheres (realms) of or around a planet.

Those who wish to proceed through the action of physical embodiment are then prepared and provided with the necessary bodies. They have an Electronic Body and around it is the Causal Body composed of whatever accumulation of qualified energy (which is all constructive) they have acquired in their journeying through the seven spheres. The I AM Presence then provides a Christ Self (Higher Mental Body) which steps down the rapid vibrations of Itself, and there is builded an etheric, mental and emotional body, each composed of the substance in which it is to function.

These are created by the Christ Self, the Builders of Form and the Beings of the elements, all working together. This process takes a very long period of time.

These Beings draw some of the finest substance of the earth element, the ethers, around a focal point of the Three-fold Flame projected by the Christ Self, into a replica of the Christ Self which forms the etheric body and is self-luminous. The (lower) mental body through which the intellectual consciousness acts, is composed of (the electronic force) the finer part of the element of air. The emotional body is composed of the finer part of the water element. It is this element that enables one to feel. The purpose of the feelings is to radiate and intensify God-qualities here in the physical world. Water forms the greatest portion of our bodies as well as of the world.

These three bodies interpenetrate each other and also interpenetrate the physical body when it has been formed. These three bodies form the inner vehicles and do not disintegrate at so-called death but remain from one embodiment to the next at inner levels and are utilized in each succeeding embodiment.

The substance of the emotional body, like the physical substance, becomes more and more solidified and dense by continually being charged with discord.

Inanimate objects are really only condensed substance and do take on qualities imposed upon them, as did the earth substance itself as well as the physical bodies.

Originally when their use had been fulfilled the electrons were returned to the universal through etherealization and not through decay and disintegration as is the case on Earth at present, which is the result of mankind's inharmony and discord.

The Christ Self projects the full self-consciousness of the Three-fold Flame into these bodies making the individual identity—man. The Seven Elohim then focus Their Flames into the intellectual consciousness anchoring them in the forehead of the etheric body.

The intellectual consciousness or outer mind is supposed to be the medium or instrument of the divine mind, for the Christ Self to work through, to contact the outer world through the senses. The senses are rays of light that proceed from the brain (a physical structure), instruments of creation for the lifestream in the world of form.

The light ray from the Presence comes into the heart and then through the brain out through the senses, but directions from the Presence are mostly contaminated by the human mind. The mind of man has become or is composed of a conglomerate mass of concepts, beliefs, thoughts and feelings, which have been drawn into the brain through sense report from the imperfections without. These predominate the actions of the average person. All senses and faculties are closely connected, especially thought and feeling, and that is how the feelings affect or influence thought so greatly.

There is not only the human mind of the individual that acts through him but there is the mass mind, an accumulation of all such matter through the centuries.

The bodies for earth life were originally created or provided for those to take embodiment, through the projection of light rays, by the parents, a masculine and feminine being, and where these rays crossed a body was created, formed to full stature, and the incoming life-stream took possession. They also retained the memory from one lifetime to the next. This means of birth still exists on other planets.

Mankind desiring to do their own will drew themselves into a density to a point where they no longer could wield the light rays and birth ceased for a time, until the present form of physical bodies was provided. The Builders of Form went and studied with great Cosmic Beings to formulate and devise the best types, structure and function of bodies that would take care of the requirements in this low vibratory action; and so the present means of birth came about. This period is what is referred to as the time of Adam and Eve. The present means of birth is to change again to the former way as the new age comes into greater manifestation.

The air element (as were the others too) was of a more rapid vibratory rate and had to be lowered (slowed down) to meet the demands of existence when the vibratory action of Earth was lowered by the discord of mankind. Aries, the Director (or shall we say, supplier) of the air element had to draw more power and lower the vibratory action of the electrons so it could be utilized by man.

The physical body, created through the present means of birth, at conception the Christ Self projects forth the Three-fold Flame (a portion of Itself) which forms the permanent atom of the heart, around which is coalesced the substance which forms the physical body. This body is formed upon the light pattern of the etheric body. It is created in accord with the keynote of the incoming lifestream; and the electrons carry its own electronic pattern.

The differences between the bodies of an unascended being and an Ascended Being are these, our mental bodies are composed of the ethers, Theirs are of living flame; our feeling worlds are composed of water, Theirs are composed of fire; our physical bodies are flesh, Theirs are bodies of fire. The purpose of physical embodiment is to become master of conditions in the world of the third dimension through the flame in the heart; by invoking it and setting the powers of the Sacred Fire into action which will manifest through the individual's world. Thus one earns the right to a fire body.

The various bodies are formed in which the Three-fold Flame may function. The Presence—God—is focalized in these bodies and gives them life. (See "The Seven Bodies" page 63.)

These bodies originally were of a much finer substance, of a more rapid vibratory rate and in harmony and balance with each other. They were similar to the present etheric substance.

A Body Elemental is assigned to each lifestream and also a Ministering Angel; these same beings stay with that individual through all embodiments.

There is drawn, before a planet is inhabited, a Manu, a World Teacher and a Maha Chohan (Who represent the three-fold action of the Godhead), there is also a Buddha. Originally These were to serve during the cycle of fourteen thousand years or the evolution of a root race.

When the time arrives for a root race to inhabit a planet the Manu draws forth approximately one seventh of His root race. The first seventh (the first sub-race) is comprised of mostly first ray individuals, those having the color blue predominating in their Causal Bodies; but He also selects some of each of the other rays. For the second cycle of two thousand years He chooses mostly those on the second ray with some of each of the other rays; and so on for each succeeding sub-race.

The Individualized Flames or lifestreams, by taking physical embodiment can develop further, and attain the fullness of the use of light. This is done by mastering creation in an atmosphere of a slower vibratory action which requires more energy to externalize form and to produce the power of radiation. This gives greater dexterity and power to the individual in his creation. Physical embodiment gives them opportunity to expand the attributes and faculties through the earth substance, to become master of energy through thought and feeling.

This gives accomplishments and added power which one who does not ever embody on a planet does not possess. The purpose of being is to gain control and mastery of the four elements through the expansion of the Flame (in the heart), and expand the Creator's kingdom; eventually becoming a Cosmic Being. The Elementals were created to be his helpers in the creation of perfection.

The mineral element, the earth substance of the physical body that is purified and raised into the Christ Self (Higher Mental Body) at the time of the Ascension and has become flame, is a part of the fire element.

The four lower bodies were meant to be always under the direct control and action of the Christ Self, but when the outer consciousness began to generate and accept human qualities, then began the separation. It is only within the substance of these bodies that it is possible for inharmony and discord to register and manifest. After a great momentum of this the outer consciousness accepted the human power as the authority and so the Christ Self withdrew or receded more and more, because there was not enough in accord with It for It to fulfill the divine plan. It would have withdrawn completely (which would have resulted in what is called "second death"), in the majority of mankind, had not Sanat Kumara come and given His assistance in sustaining the Three-fold Flame in the hearts of mankind through all these many, many centuries of time.

Some individuals did not permit themselves to be

drawn into the human or discordant actions at this time, but held to the light and original plan. Therefore, they made the Ascension instead and some are now great Cosmic Beings Who are an authority for mankind and Earth. Those going the opposite way have gone so far that they believe and accept themselves an entity—an identity apart from the Source, which has been completely forgotten by some, the outer selves taking all credit to themselves. The difference is simply the result of the use of the attention. A Cosmic Being, the Divine Director, said that He was at that time unascended and rendering a service similar to the Messengers, that He warned the people then as to what the attention could do, but they would not believe it. The need now is to become and remain humble to the Light—the Great Ones, and positive to all that is of the human. It must be a humility deep in the feelings.

Our own world is a duplication of the creation of a universe.

The beings of the elements prepared the planet for habitation. After this came the Angelic Host whose service it is to radiate Their qualities to the mankind coming to inhabit this orb. The Angelic Host are taken to a planet by the Archangels before it is inhabited by the race.

Mankind, angels and elementals work in conscious co-operation with each other. Thus the three kingdoms or evolutions have opportunity for development on each planet. All these are guarded by the Seven Archangels.

Man is to become co-Creator with God, a master power; the angels and elementals are to render service unto him and give obedience to him.

The Seven Archangels represented the seven Rays at the beginning of habitation on Earth as Chohans.

When a planet is to be inhabited it is made known amongst other planets that there is opportunity for life-streams to serve. Those desiring to serve in such capacity are known as guardians. These guardians already have much development and are volunteered from other more advanced planets. They go with the Manu and give assistance to the new race.

The Manu of the first root race with the guardians and the ones of the first sub-race to come forth in the beginning of habitation on Earth were led and escorted by Archangel Michael in the descent and it was at the time of the Spring solstice. The location where they descended was in the vicinity of the Teton Mountains in the United States of America.

A planet has an approximate cycle of evolution for its races. The Earth's cycle was to be seven root races with seven sub-races in each. A sub-race was to cover a cycle of two thousand years, as one of each of the seven rays predominated in that cycle, which was to nourish one particular center within the physical and inner bodies. This gives an approximate cycle of fourteen thousand years to a root race, in which time mankind were to attain mastery.

There were the two golden ages referred to as the Garden of Eden. There was no dissonance and no static in the atmosphere then. The first and second root races completed their course on schedule. The third was a little longer in the process but did attain the eternal freedom in the Ascension, and has returned 'Home". There was no division of races in the beginning.

It was during the progress of the fourth root race, about the middle of this cycle (which was the middle of Earth's natural progress), that at a Cosmic Council it was decided for the Earth to take on the laggards from other planets. These laggards were individuals who were stranded and without a planet on which to embody to complete their evolution. Evidently some were from various other planets; those who had failed to make the grade when their planet progressed into a higher state of being. However, it was said that there was a planet called Mal-Dec, which we call Lucifer, that was destroyed through discord and the release of atomic energy, that way leaving several billion lifestreams without a planet, since they had generated too much discord or were not developed sufficiently to be given their Ascension at the time of that crisis.

Taking on the laggards has overcrowded our planet as well as drawn mankind and guardians into discord and this density we are in now. The Earth was originally designed for around three and one half billion lifestreams with only a portion of these in embodiment at one time.

There are still many of the fourth root race on Earth, some of the fifth, a small number of the sixth, and at this writing, the seventh is beginning to come in.

There were magnificent Temples of the various virtues manifest on Lemuria at the time. The high priests were notified of the decision to take on these laggards. They went into action to prepare for the event by making application and drawing forth more power and light. This preparation went on for around one hundred years. Only certain ones in the Temples were informed about this, the populace did not know of it.

The time came and the laggards began to take embodiment; they coming through these individuals who were embodied on Earth, living in an innocent and pure state.

All requirements were supplied by/through precipitation, as man was not ordained to labor, to earn a living by the sweat of the brow as is the condition presently. The density of the physical body is the reason for it and the struggle which mankind has, because that density which is produced by discord in the feelings does not let the energy from the Presence flow through freely. Man came here a being of light, free. The Earth was provided for him, beautiful with all that was required; with Elementals to produce every good thing in nature. There were no storms and weather conditions to combat or the need of protection from them. Therefore, present day conditions of materialism were not required. Life-streams came here to learn to direct and master energy for definite manifestation; not just to provide for the function of living.

The conditions became more and more discordant and of a destructive nature instead of constructive, as many of the laggards who had greatly developed intellectual powers and selfish desires and purposes, focused the attention of the intellect upon sense appetites through subtle feelings. They got into governmental and other key positions and in that way influenced great numbers. Some also had the power to draw into embodiment individuals of their own nature and who would work in cooperation with them. Thus came about the "fall of man", confusion, forgetfulness of their Source and disintegration.

It is said it was during that time animal creation (imperfect creatures) on Earth began; and that there were no animals in the first golden ages.

It is because of mankind's misqualified energy that animals have destructive natures and are vicious. They take on these impure radiations, and this same action is the cause of blight, fungus growth, poisonous and distorted plants.

Animals are elemental beings functioning in bodies, most of them with horizontal instead of upright spines, and unpleasant radiations.

Beings of the four elements are created by Cosmic Beings. Their nature is to imitate, mirror or take on what they see and become that form; of course in the beginning that produced only perfection when there were no imperfect thought forms and distortions. Therefore, when mankind began to generate these human qualities, the beings of the elements seeing them, also began to out-picture them.

Through that process many of them became karmically attached to certain lifestreams. Some of these individuals became what is termed black magicians and they deliberately compelled beings of the elements to take on and inhabit animal forms/bodies, so they could hold their focus among mankind on Earth. That way the animals were used as warriors against mankind, especially those desiring to progress in the light. Remember the beings of the elements were vowed to serve life—individuals with the Three-fold Flame in their hearts.

The so-called black magicians at one time even had schools. There was one such school before the sinking of Mu where some three hundred of them congregated in a cave (a city) in the Andes in South America (which is still there). They created various animal forms out of the substance in the atmosphere which had been qualified with discord, and compelled elemental beings into them.

However, the Light is always more powerful and there is the action of the great Law that when destructive forces reach a certain point the Law takes a hand. This is done through Ascended and Cosmic Beings. That way the school was broken up and never again was such a focus or action permitted.

Life is extremely generous and kind and always gives opportunity to reverse a wrong. When this focus or school was broken up the black magicians were given opportunity to withdraw their destructive creations including their animal creations, but they refused. Therefore, the animals have remained as such to this day.

Many black magicians and lifestreams have gone through what is called "second death" and some of their creations continued to exist and function. Some redemption has taken place through humanity's love, and through that, animals have been domesticated.

Animals have ganglionic centers and emotional bodies but plant life does not. It is life energy that beats the heart of animals, not an Individualized Flame of God as is the case in mankind. Within the heart of these imprisoned elementals is the pattern which they once were and are to become again.

Group souls are the combined consciousness of each species, with an Angel Deva (who has volunteered) as the directing intelligence and guardian, holding the perfect concept for each. It is mostly angels who volunteered to render this service.

Elemental life in animal form grew thick skins, horns, hoofs, shells and scales as a protection, a defense mechanism, against the currents of viciousness they felt in the atmosphere about them. Plant life developed thorns, poison and heavy bark for the same reason. The cactus is a distortion of plant life, caused by inharmony and the many human qualities.

These protective activities will disappear as mankind, nature and all on Earth again become harmonious, and discordant feelings are replaced by love. All animal life has to be redeemed, and that is done by love, it will come mostly through the Angelic Host.

The octopus was once a radiating being, instead of those arms there were rays of light. The oyster was a beautiful little being of purity, a focus of the Goddess of Purity and that is the reason for the pearl there today, which is a remnant of that action. Bugs, insects, vermin and disease germs are just condensed thought forms; they are composed of the discordant qualities generated by mankind.

Birds come under another action. They were created by the Ascended Masters as messengers to mankind. Some have, however, taken on human qualities which accounts for their destructive activities.

An animal's loyalty to its master can well be attributed to the fact that it is an elemental being.

Many people today are very attached to animals because of karmic debt. Humanity in general loves the animals which is well and good, but they have an attachment with them through the emotional body. This too is not freedom and must be corrected.

Animals have to be redeemed from these forces and conditions in which they function and enter again into their natural state of existence and progress in evolution. Some ancient animals are extinct, evidently having been redeemed.

When an animal is killed the flesh registers fear and

that is absorbed into the emotional body of those eating it. The reasons for not eating meat and using serums should be apparent. The use of alcohol, narcotics and tobacco should be avoided also.

It is well known that a Master can go amongst vicious animals; what takes place is the radiation from the Master transmutes those qualities in the animal. Usually soon after that something happens which releases the life from that form, setting it free, because it has been redeemed.

Deserts were created by discord and the release of atomic bombs and such like; and nature even to this day has refused to grow vegetation there. They are to again become fertile and beautiful as gardens.

The present density which is caused by imperfection and discord, came about very gradually over a very long period of time. The imperfection, the wrong or human qualities which had been generated by the laggards then embodying on Earth very subtly through radiation and contagion, began to enter the mental and feeling worlds of the pure lifestreams; many of the guardians as well as the evolving race.

The destructive forces released by mankind had their beginning through human beings, by their determination to assert authority (over others). This momentum was gained by the attention and use of energy by their own desire only, with no assistance from any other source, and it was a long time before it was even perceptible.

The lowest ebb or darkest time of Earth was before Sanat Kumara came, when the Cosmic Council of the Suns of the solar systems voted for the dissolution of the Earth. Sanat Kumara attended that Council and afterwards decided to come and sustain the Earth; He then got permission to do so from the Council. The call had gone forth by Archangel Raphael for more guardians. Then Sanat Kumara and others came. The use of fire, lost to the masses, was again established. Previous to this there was a time when there were only four individuals holding the connection with the higher realms. There have been times when there was only one.

There was created and established the Karmic Board previous to Sanat Kumara's coming; the generation of discord brought about this requirement.

The principle qualities which are the cause of discord are condemnation, criticism and judgment.

Imperfection is a rate of vibration slower than or below a certain point. The rates of vibration that produce perfection do not go below that point; there is a dividing line. The motive behind the action or use of a thing is a very important factor and it can and does often determine whether it is good or evil, perfect or imperfect. It is sometimes stressed that opposition is necessary to progress; that is not so, because on other planets they make progress without having opposition by human actions and qualities. There is certain natural resistance which promotes and stimulates progress but this is all harmonious.

Some of the priests (of Lemuria) who had never wanted the laggards to come, began to make application to have them taken off the Earth, instead of being willing to apply the Law to sublimate and transmute the misqualified energies and redeem them. That brought about a division in the priesthood, whereas had they stayed unified the sinking of the continent would not have taken place.

All this eventually brought about the sinking of Lemuria, which sank over night with some sixty million people. The focus of discord which was the beginning of the destruction that finally sank the continent was located near San Diego, California. There the etheric record of the ancient city was seen at a cosmic moment one evening in nineteen thirty-four by many people passing by on the highway at that time.

Where Europe is now, at the time of Mu, there were thirteen states, twelve states and the key-state which was what is now Switzerland. It represented wisdom, the gold plume of the Three-fold Flame; France, love, the pink plume; England, power, the blue plume. When the laggards came to Earth, one with a powerful momentum of destructive qualities embodied, in what is now Siberia. He lived many lifetimes there and drew through occult knowledge others of his own character who would cooperate with him. They got into governmental and important positions, thereby influencing great numbers of people. Thus was built an accumulation of force which sank the continent. (The tops of the Alps remained because of the purity of that state.) Europe was raised again when Atlantis sank. Some of the same lifestreams re-embodied there again many times, creating similar conditions as before. When the destructive forces in Siberia got so very great they were counteracted by the great Law by an action of sudden freezing. The influence of those actions of the former age, especially the three-fold action, can even now be seen in those particular countries of Europe today.

There is however, the action of the great Law which is always more powerful when held to than human qualities and actions or creations.

The Earth is functioning in vibratory action because of the discord on it, below or outside the periphery of the seven spheres instead of within it.

The psychic or astral strata (planes) or realms consist of the misqualified and destructive energy in and around mankind and the Earth; but there are no gradations as is sometimes claimed. However, certain qualities do hover more closely to the surface of Earth than others. This is not a plane (place) to dwell in or develop on or in but to be avoided completely. One should go through it protected by his Pillar of Light, like going through a tunnel of light. The psychic realm is between us and the seventh sphere, since no discord or imperfection may be allowed to enter the realms of perfection (heaven), the discord has been compelled to remain outside that realm and is held around the Earth by a wall of light.

The curses placed on jewels, tombs, families and houses have been sustained for centuries and have acted from time to time. These were a direct action of the power of invocation for destructive purposes and actions. This destructive practice began on Lemuria and has come down through the ages and has manifested in various forms, such as the voodoo practices in Africa, witchcraft, hexes and other destructive incantations. Sometimes these things are thought to be imaginery but they are more than that. They are elemental life (energy) acting in obedience to the directions of a fiat or decree. Energy is a certain form of elemental life. With the incoming of the Seventh Ray, the ray of invocation these things can now be reversed, and that elemental life released, purified and re-polarized.

The divine plan to be outpictured here is lowered through the seven spheres. It manifests just as ideas in the first sphere or realm; in the second sphere it takes form; in the third sphere they are energized and become living things on the inner which can be externalized in the outer world to bring about perfection and bless mankind. Then the Beings of the fourth sphere through light rays project ideas of a certain nature into the consciousness of receptive individuals embodied on the planet which become ideas in their minds (especially of architecture and music); the Beings in the fifth sphere give ideas along scientific lines to indivduals, and work through those human beings; from the sixth sphere the Beings work with and through embodied individuals interested in ministry, missionary work and such like. The seventh sphere is closest to Earth and is well supplied with ideas, patterns and plans of perfection of every kind which are ready to be made manifest here on Earth.

When an idea is projected forth into the atmosphere

of Earth from the higher realms or even from another human being, it can register or be picked up from the ethers by any person's mind which is attuned. That is the reason as it has happened at times, that more than one person may write the same type of a story, yet neither took it from the other.

Some people have developed the psychic sight which is a partial action of the All-Seeing Eye, therefore not wholly dependable, as is the All-Seeing Eye. Prophets get their prophecies by tuning into the etheric (akashic) records and observing there the causes set up which, of course, outpicture under the law of cause and effect unless they are transmuted by some one understanding the Cosmic Law and calling into action the I AM Presence, the Ascended and Cosmic Beings, by which means those wrong actions can be transmuted and replaced by constructive actions to produce perfection. Mankind's attention on these predicted events and dwelling on them even helps bring them into manifestation. That is why the Ascended Ones have stressed to avoid prophecies given by human beings.

Now that the change is taking place, with a minimized cataclysmic action, it does not mean that all prophecies which had been predicted were just imagination. Those predictions were based on causes existing at the time and are derived by reading the etheric records. However, through the knowledge of the I AM Presence and with sufficient understanding of the Law by a small number of mankind (the students) making application and working in cooperation with the Ascended Ones to fulfill Their (divine) plan, is enabling the change of the axis to take place, the melting of the ice caps and the raising of the continents without the tremendous cataclysmic action which would otherwise have resulted.

It is only now that the Cosmic Wheel is changing, for which the Silent Watcher has waited two hundred thousand years.

Therefore through sufficient cooperation with the great Law and the Great Ones, instead of going down with the continent (singing a farewell song) as was the case with Lemuria (Mu), it is possible to keep the continents from sinking and thereby save the lives of many millions of people who would otherwise go out and have to take embodiment again, to finish their course on Earth. There does however, still have to be change—a change of consciousness, which has to come before the new age with all its perfections can be fully established.

The information was given in nineteen thirty-nine that there had been formed a so-called "compound" into which many dis-embodied individuals were taken from the atmosphere of Earth; especially the intellectual and advanced ones who had gotten on the wrong track. This way they could no longer influence the people of Earth. They were not desirous of complying with the cosmic law of progress of this universe and therefore could not be taken to the realms of light.

There have been established Temples and Focuses of the Violet Flame in recent years in the etheric realm and lower atmosphere of Earth, which will help clear the psychic realm. All the disembodied have been taken care of in these Temples and schoolrooms.

There has also been established, over every continent a focus of the Violet Flame or cauldron which is like a lake of fire into which mankind are drawn in their inner bodies while asleep.

The destructive individuals that leave the Earth through so-called death, are taken to the schoolrooms and temples which have been established in the etheric realms of Earth. The difference now is that they are not allowed to remain inactive or just follow their destructive impulses as was the case formerly because of free will. The Law has only within the last twenty years allowed that free will to be set aside. They must now devote a minimum of one hour per day to application, one hour to studying and one hour in rendering service. These temples and foci did not exist in the lower realms before and destructive individuals just existed in the atmosphere of Earth in their (lower) inner bodies.

There were ancient civilizations where the Gobi and Sahara Deserts are now. These declined because of becoming overrun by hordes, which were the laggards from other planets.

The civilization which reached its height about two hundred thousand years ago was one of the greatest on Earth.

The Punch Bowl on the present Hawaiian Islands was a great focus of light on Mu, which was then on one of the highest mountain ranges. Another range crossed this one or rather they came together in "T" fashion, at this point. This focus of love, harmony and purity still has its effect on the people there to this day. The peaks of these mountain ranges remained above water when Mu sank. The cataclysm two hundred thousand years ago caused these ranges to be raised to their greatest height. The tops of these were blown off during the cataclysm around twelve thousand years ago, which formed the Hawaiian Islands. They were active volcanoes until Jesus' ministry, at which time they became nearly inactive through the great release of Divine Love during His service and Ascension.

The changing and counteracting of the gas belts through the understanding and application of this Law will make them completely inactive (it is hoped), as well as change conditions in other parts of the world.

The southern half of the state of Texas was under water and during the cataclysm which took place about eighty thousand years ago it was raised. About ten thousand years later a great focus of light was drawn there and a great civilization came forth in which Saint Germain was a big factor. Contact with the Ascended Ones was maintained during that civilization.

Where the Sahara Desert is now there was a great and marvelous civilization which reached its height around seventy thousand years ago. It was one of the greatest. That area was fertile land and semi-tropical in climate. Its ruler was the beloved Saint Germain with mostly advanced lifestreams in embodiment. The government of the people consisted of seven departments, one for each ray, with two lesser Masters on each ray, and they were under the direct supervision of fourteen Ascended Masters. The people knew of and had contact with their own God-Presence. Had the people continued to give obedience and maintained harmony it could have become a nation of Ascended Masters and the Earth would have gone forth into perfection and all the failures of civilization and war since would have been unknown. The time came when the ruler, who was the only one who possessed the wisdom and power to such a great degree, had to be withdrawn under cosmic law. A large banquet was given to which all the king's councilors with their staffs (over 500) were invited. A drink of liquid light, an elixir, was given each one present. This drink gave a protection to the lifestreams which held them to the light through the centuries. Saint Germain (the ruler) asked for this and it was given from the Ascended Masters' Realm by the Cosmic Being known as the Divine Director.

The Atlantean civilization came after the sinking of Mu. It was on the continent of Atlantis which was a stretch of land between Central America and Europe. This civilization reached great heights; many taking embodiment were lifestreams having advanced knowledge and attainment.

The priesthood, some of them the same ones as on Lemuria, again divided, reproducing the same condition as had occurred before. Again on Atlantis was an age when it was hoped would be permanent, thereby providing a harmonious condition on Earth for the development of all future races. The priesthood warned the people of the pending cataclysm, which held the interest and their consideration for a time but after a few years it had been forgotten, except by the true student and aspirant. Some of the priesthood became intellectual, proud, arrogant and so versed in the letter of the law that they lost the true spiritual values. Thus was the door closed to real inspiration or direction from the Ascended Masters. (It was this kind of a priesthood that crucified Jesus.) These priests swayed the people. There remained only a few priests who held to the true spiritual activity. Then again in Egypt many of the same lifestreams were responsible for her downfall.

The people's disobedience and the misuse of their creative faculties and wrong use of energy, and the use of the atomic bomb, again on Atlantis, brought about the submerging of nearly all of the continent. During the cataclysmic action around fourteen thousand years ago the central and principal part, a small portion remained which formed the Island called Poseidonis. This is when the Great Lakes came into existence.

Both India and China had great civilizations during this period (of Atlantis), also at the time Poseidonis sank. These two countries have maintained their identity through several civilizations, which no other countries have done. This is due to the Retreats in the Himalayan Mountains and the Masters both ascended and unascended Who work there and maintain Their foci of light. At the time before Mu sank much of the light was transferred to India and China where it has been guarded; it is now being transferred to the Western hemisphere. Some of the records and treasures have already been taken to the Teton, Lake Titicaca and other Retreats for the incoming age.

Europe was raised again when Atlantis sank; it had gone down when Mu sank. Saint Germain tried in his last embodiment, in England and later through Napoleon, to bring about a United States of Europe on a similar plan of that which existed ages before.

The country around the Amazon River between twelve and fourteen thousand years ago was at an altitude of around five thousand feet and was semi-tropical, all this was changed during the last cataclysm around twelve thousand years ago. This action submerged the cities there, widened the mouth of the Amazon and changed the east and west coast lines of the continent. A marvelous civilization had existed there with Casimir Poseidon as the ruler.

Meru was the name of the continent. It was named after Lord Meru Whose Focus is near Lake Titicaca.

This civilization and that on Atlantis, had power boxes in which was generated their power from the universal light. These civilizations and also the one on Mu, had airships which far transcended anything we have today.

Then there was a civilization which was known as the

Pirua, after which came the Inca civilization in South America with a colony in Mexico. The majority of people who embodied there were similar to the American Indians, but those at the head of the government were advanced lifestreams. Fourteen from the Etheric City over the Sahara Desert came to assist the Inca ruler. One of these was Saint Germain.

These civilizations covered a period of thousands of years.

Beloved Saint Germain endeavored to raise a whole province of people on Poseidonis into the ascended state. He had brought them to the point where all their requirements were precipitated for them. They did not have to work for anything. This was done not through their own attainment but from the power and focus held by Saint Germain.

There was very great development in mechanics. They had much greater perfection in airships than there is at present, with air-transportation all over the world.

They had become aware of their I AM Presence but through disobedience and rebellion in the feelings which acted because the Law had not allowed the use of the Transmuting Violet Flame to be given in the outer world, Saint Germain was compelled to withdraw. Out of one hundred twenty million people, less than fifty thousand listened to the warning of destruction ahead. Poseidonis sank during cataclysmic action over twelve thousand years ago, some sixty million people sinking with it. The highest peaks of the mountain ranges are now the Azores and Madeira Islands. This deluge is what is referred to as the "Flood" in the Bible. The wild men in the Himalayan Mountains and elsewhere are remnants from the last cataclysm, so it was said.

The Ascended and Cosmic Beings preserved buildings, records, formulas and whatever They wished to keep, by hermetically sealing them at the bottom of the Atlantic Ocean. They will bring these forth in the new age just ahead. It was said that parts of a buried city can be seen from an airplane off the peninsula Yucatan. Before the sinking of Poseidonis this knowledge was taken to Egypt and carried down through the priesthood. One hundred boats (each with forty or more persons) left the continent at a particular time before its sinking; each boat carried a portion of some specific Flame from the Temple that specialized in that virtue. They went in various directions towards their appointed destiny. All were lost except ten which arrived in Mexico, Peru, Easter Islands, Egypt at Luxor, and some in Asia. These priests and devotees then lived at those locations unto the end of that lifetime, returning many times in future embodiments. They remembered the requirements of the priests and priestesses and therefore the law and disciplines were not written out as now. This only started when the light was getting very dim before the time of Moses; it reached its lowest ebb, since Atlantean Days when Jesus came which turned the tide.

This great assistance of the Ascended Masters and

Cosmic Beings which is now being given again was not done since before Poseidonis sank.

Priests and priestesses had the knowledge and use of the Sacred Fire to the point where the Flame was visible, in many civilizations; particularly in the one around two hundred thousand years ago, the one on Atlantis and the one on the Amazon.

There were a number of Temples on Mu and Atlantis each specializing in a certain activity or virtue. Priests, priestesses and people from all over the world came to these Temples for instruction, assistance, radiation and re-charge of that particular quality.

There were Temples on Atlantis where various cities are now, each manifesting a specific quality. Where New York City (Manhattan Island) is, there were twelve Temples around a central one, known as the Temples of the Sun, wherein was the Liberty Flame. The Temple with the action of protection was where Philadelphia is now; at the location of Denver was a Temple dedicated to the elementals; where San Francisco is, was a city of the seven hills with the Temple to the Seven Elohim. Where Los Angeles is there was a Temple to the Angels and before the cataclysm fourteen thousand years ago in that Temple the Angels were visible to those serving there. There has always been a Temple of Silence in every golden age.

There was a civilization in Egypt which rose to a great height. This was due to the action of the Ascension Flame there. The people were developed individuals and there was tremendous intellectual accomplishment, also the greatest corrupt priesthood known. The misuse of their knowledge and power brought about the fall of that civilization.

Later the Roman Empire rose to great heights but also went down. Jesus came to Earth at the low ebb of mankind's spirituality and through His mission the currents on the inner were reversed, setting into action the Divine—the Christ within the individual, which started mankind on an up-grade toward the freedom for all.

It was said that there have been six golden ages and six major cataclysms. These occurred around a million years ago, eight hundred thousand years ago, two hundred thousand years ago, one hundred twenty thousand years ago, eighty thousand years ago and fourteen thousand years ago. Then there was a smaller one over twelve thousand years ago when the Island of Poseidonis sank.

A change of the poles takes place during cataclysmic activity, but that is always governed by great Intelligent Beings.

ASCENDED MASTERS, COSMIC AND DIVINE BEINGS

It is essential that students realize that there is a conscious Being back of any intelligent activity; whether it is a metaphysical aspect of spirit or any virtue or action of the seven rays. The spirit or divine qualities are sustained and directed by intelligent Beings, of the Legions of Light.

The Legions of Light in a broad sense include all Beings of light—the Ascended Masters, Cosmic Beings, Devas, Divine Beings, Seraphim, Cherubim, Angelic Host and Beings of the Elements. In a specific sense a Legion can be all Those serving with or under the direction of some Great Being. That would be His Legion or Legions.

Great Beings are behind prayer, invocation and decrees. They are the Ascended Masters, Cosmic Beings, Angelic Host, Beings of the Elements and all Divine Beings. They are the invisible power which produces manifestations out here.

The tremendous accomplishments that have resulted from this understanding and cooperative service of students with the Divine Beings is proof that there must be response and direction from this realm through which the Law acts, or in order for it to act.

The Great White Brotherhood is composed of these Beings. Certain Ones of These form the Spiritual Hierarchy for the human kingdom of which the Lord of the World is an authority. Each One of the Hierarchy has a specific service to the Earth and its evolutions.

It must be understood that these great Beings carry on many other creative activities and render services of various types (some of great Cosmic import) besides these referred to here, which are Their particular services to or in connection with mankind and Earth. While They are rendering service They are also developing and making progress Themselves. There is always greater consciousness to attain to, and no matter how high a Being goes there is always a Teacher serving in a higher capacity.

Life—the Law has given or appointed certain Masters as the authority and dominion over a given quality, activity or service, therefore certain things come under His jurisdiction and no other Master interferes with that nor do They do Each Other's work.

The Ascended Masters have through the ages protected mankind in many ways; particularly from destroying themselves through their inventions and use of destructive power, machines and weapons. It may be likened to the protection of children by their parents or guardians who keep them from a hot stove to avoid their burning themselves.

These Beings can do for us what we cannot do for ourselves, and They are willing and happy to do it. The law must be complied with, which is that recognition and acceptance must come from mankind or the one to be benefited. The Masters are permitted to give this assistance through the expanding power released into outer action by the student through his love for his own I AM Presence and the Ascended Masters. Therefore, it is necessary to cognize and become aware of these Divine Beings, Their activities and special service of each One to mankind and the Earth.

This is a practical working principle of this instruction. The Ascended Masters are so necessary to mankind's attainment because They have the feeling of attainment.

The various Great Beings have come forth from time to time to release whatever qualities mankind could utilize.

When mankind no longer desired these God qualities but instead pursued in the opposite direction, the Beings Who represented these qualities had to recede and thus entered the Great Silence. They remained there as far as Earth was concerned and have only now come forth at the call of some of mankind (the students). Some Beings have served and worked for mankind's benefit unknown to them through the ages and are only now being given any recognition.

Cosmic Beings as a rule work at cosmic levels and seldom descend into lower realms of action, or the dealing with individuals. However, during the past twenty years They have done so to a great extent, during this time of extreme effort to save the planet.

To know the other Ascended Masters and Divine Beings Who have offered Their special qualities at this time as well as Those Who are known, is the great need of mankind and the solution to their problems and world conditions. To solve world problems we have to go beyond psychology which is the science of the human mind, and with mind is feeling, intricately woven into it. The solutions are only found in the divine mind. The Ascended Masters have these past twenty years endeavored to create a closeness of feeling from the students towards Them. Therefore, They have given so much information concerning the various Ascended and Divine Beings. Some students of other teachings object to this, feeling it is worshiping the Masters too much. Yet the purpose is to generate in the students the *feeling of the reality* of Them, instead of having only an abstract concept of Them. To just look to spirit is not enough. Spirit is radiation. What they get from spirit is because of radiation of some One or more of these Beings. They tune into that, but that does not mean they have direct contact with a certain Being. What they get comes from radiation or from etheric records, or even entities.

Each of the various teachings of the past gives a certain amount of Truth, usually one aspect. Thus mental concepts and orthodoxy (through fear, bigotry, et cetera) were allowed to hold the minds of those interested on only that particular phase of Truth instead of letting them expand in consciousness in other phases too. The Cosmic Law is now that every one's Christ Self shall take command of the outer self and be the Christ in action, instead of there being just an avatar there should be many Christus manifest, many who attain Christhood.

The Ascended Ones have through the dictations and addresses held a direct connection with the Earth and released the light to the people for the expansion of the light which had to come in order for the Earth to survive. It was said that this is the greatest Truth brought forth in more than four hundred thousand years.

A dream is the remembrance of some experiences or parts of them on awakening, which took place at inner levels in one's finer bodies. Yes, they are real, even more real than this physical world, but usually only portions are retained. Most of the time these are perverted.

A visitation is not a dream. It is the Presence of a Being from the inner realms to an individual while fully conscious; perceptible to his outer sense consciousness, and a transformation takes place within himself. The action of that transformation is that the light and power of the Being which is of a much higher rate of vibration than the atoms of the individual (human being) consumes, transmutes the discord in those atoms of the physical as well as in the emotional, mental and etheric bodies and raises the vibratory action. Each atom consists of tiny intelligences whose nature it is to mimic or become a replica, therefore they take on the perfection of that Being present which results in the transformation.

Saul of Tarsus, later known as Paul the Apostle, had a visitation by Jesus that transformed his life. To Moses appeared the Great Angel, in the burning bush, as it is recorded; the burning bush refers to His radiance. A visitation also took place with Joseph Smith who founded the Mormon movement. The experiences upon which it is based, he had through a visitation or contact with One of the Great Ones; Who gave him certain aspects or principles of the law, which is the foundation for their teaching. Archangel Michael and Others came to Mary, the Mother of Jesus, which sustained her through the very difficult life she had.

Many of these Ascended Masters had it much more difficult in their attainment than the action under the great LAW now. There was not permitted then the tremendous assistance which is now being given by the Ascended Masters, Cosmic Beings and Angelic Host. They had to hide in caves or some secluded place and then try to draw forth the actions of the Sacred Fire, without the knowledge of their own I AM Presence or the promptings from the Ascended Ones. They then experimented with what they could draw forth, as to what results they could produce, in divine alchemy et cetera. They had only the promptings from within the Flame in their own hearts as to whether they were on the right track or had gotten into black magic.

There are many here from other planets who have taken embodiment through the centuries. They came as guardians of the race (those evolving on Earth). Some were very far advanced but have been drawn into the density along with mankind. Some have made the Ascension from this planet and are now a part of the Hierarchy of the Earth.

The great Cosmic Beings were the creators of the occult laws and the previous teachings are today only about thirty-five per cent as originally given.

How does one know the (Ascended) Masters are real? It is known through inner perception; some may refer to it as psychic. There is a difference between the two, and to clarify that mankind need the assistance of the Ascended Ones.

The Ascended Masters will clothe the students in a garment, a radiance and that makes the students a part of Them.

An Ascended Master can of course enfold one in His Flame and make him or her victorious. This would be only temporary unless that one has called his I AM Presence into action first, to correct the condition, and make progress. When the I AM Presence has been set into action through the individual's command and the Master enfolds him in His Flame then that becomes permanent. Then at the recognition and acceptance of the Presence with the attention on the Master's quality. it can be felt and activated.

The Ascended Ones will give us Their qualities and momentum but to have them we must accept them, which is more than just decreeing for them. The mind and feelings must be stilled to the point where those qualities can enter our feelings and in contemplation we accept them. This is one phase of application not always understood.

For efficacy in conscious invocation and decreeing the feeling must be convinced and follow the pattern of words and thought. The power of feeling charged into the decree determines its efficacy at inner levels as well as in outer manifestation. A decree made silently that is charged with a positive feeling and confidence is more powerful than shouting when it is without the confirmation of the feelings.

When the Ascended Masters stop the action of destructive forces in and around an individual by the projection of a light ray, the circle of blue flame or the action of the cross of blue flame, They are not interfering in any way with the free will of that individual. They are simply stopping the action of the destructive force and holding it in abeyance; the individual is still free to choose how he shall act. Destructive forces do interfere with free will but when they are made inactive and that pressure is removed, the individual is more apt to choose right actions.

When one has accepted the I AM Presence and when the karma of misqualified energy has been transmuted, this *will* give that one a power increased thirty or forty times.

Ascended Masters and Cosmic Beings are one with God but with conditions of different quality or degree of activity.

The Ascended Ones and Beings of pure light are free from the gravity pull of Earth. They move through space at will by Their Own intelligence directed through thought and by Their Own power generated by Themselves. Gravity pull is a certain power put into a planet by its creators to hold it together and to hold its evolutions upon it.

The Hierarchy of a planet consists of some Cosmic Beings Who give Their Cosmic assistance to that planet. Many of Those serving in this capacity have ascended from that planet and the natural progression is that as others ascend They take the place of or step into positions of the Hierarchy and Those Who held that position go on into greater service and development. That has, however, not been entirely true with the Earth in its discordant state. Some Beings have vowed to stay and serve until the Earth is redeemed and all free, and some were required to stay for this reason. There is the action of the Law that a teacher is to some degree responsible for the instruction he gives out and how it is used by his pupil or student. Therefore he (the Teacher) has an obligation to Life—the Law, until that is made right. There are some in the present Hierarchy of Earth Who come within this category, Whose students failed on the "Path" and some even became what is termed black magicians.

"God" and "Lord" are used as titles of respect. The words imply a Being Who has made the Ascension, having become *one* with God in action; Lord signifies one having become the Law. Lord is practically synonymous with Law. It was once said that the particular action of a Goddess was with substance while that of a Being designated as a God was that of flame action.

An Ascended Master's picture is the best (or greatest), the most potent focus He has of Himself in the outer world. They are at present particularly, using Their pictures (even though portrayals are not perfect), as a means of radiation and connection of consciousness with Their chelas (students). Their names also are a means of connection although the name is not the Being; but it serves as a sort of bridge to make connection with that One, especially at mankind's present level of consciousness. In the higher states of consciousness a name is not necessary. Music also helps make connection and attunement. Each lifestream has a particular melody or certain music which is termed his cosmic keynote. Some of these keynotes are held within or are similar to certain melodies or pieces of music we have on Earth.

The Ascended Masters endeavor to keep alive, and stimulate the flame of divinity and the God qualities within the people of Earth. They are the guardians of the Sacred Fire.

Some description of Individual Divine Beings will be given but of course there are many other Beings working for mankind's freedom.

Each One of These Who is brought to your attention manipulates a particular quality or a special activity for the blessing of mankind.

The Ascended Masters are willing to give assistance and as They are presented, you may feel a response. There may be a greater response from certain Ones than from Others. This may be due to former association or because of the ray you are on or your capacity to accept.

May this now be an introduction to the Beings you have not previously heard of; while reading *feel* you are *meeting* Them.

This teaching, and working in cooperation with the Great White Brotherhood has been the key that unlocked the door into cosmic action for mankind and the Earth. We might compare it, for example, to the power at Boulder Dam. All one has to do there, to light great areas, is flip a switch or push a button. Now in getting acquainted with the Hierarchy, the various Ascended Masters and Beings of Light, and working with Them is like moving, walking on an escalator. We make some effort, but are as a whole going ahead far beyond our own effort. Such has been these past twenty or more years— and still there is opportune time.

This understanding will help bring in the new age which is to be the last and permanent age on Earth.

The Sacred Fire is life—primal life that has been qualified by Intelligent Beings. It is qualified with the various qualities and activities that produce perfection. Each individual is free to qualify life, and he has a certain amount of results.

Now we have the opportunity and privilege to use not only what we *can* qualify but we may call forth and use that which is already so qualified by Great Beings, and thereby have a power and momentum of centuries of accumulation. All this as a gift from the Divine Beings. This, one can have by the acceptance of the Ascended Masters and making the call. For example, in the use of the Transmuting Violet Flame, when one is going to use only that which he qualifies, he may not have much results; but if he draws forth that Violet Flame which is already prepared to act, to cleanse and purify, it is in effect like a cleaning fluid one can buy in the store. If one would have to work out the formula for the cleaning fluid, how much results would the average person get? Likewise if he is going to have to work out the correct blending of primal life of some activities of purity, mercy and love in proper proportions to create an action of transmutation (the Violet Flame, a spiritual cleanser), he might not get much accomplished.

The vibratory action of not only Earth but the other planets and systems of this universe or scheme is being stepped up, becoming more rapid in order to take the step forward. The four lower bodies of mankind likewise must increase the frequency of their vibrations, that is, the electrons of which they are composed must become more rapid in vibratory action; under Cosmic Law it is not a matter of free will as before, but it must be done. Previously individuals on various planets could, through free will, refuse to accelerate their own inner bodies and that way they became laggards when their planets went forward; but from what was said this is not the case this time.

The conditions have been all through the ages that an individual seeking the light might spend a whole lifetime just pilgrimaging to one focus of light or a Master somewhere on Earth. He might get there and he might not. Now the Cosmic Command is that all must come into the light and understanding of the Law, therefore under the Cosmic Law the Masters are coming to the students instead, to give this assistance and instruction through the dictations and addresses.

The New Age is to be the era of *freedom*. What does freedom mean to mankind? It is a getting away from or an absence of the limiting and discordant conditons, which are manifestations of the negative aspect of the Law. Real freedom comes in the positive aspect of the Law which is the conscious use of the fire element—the Sacred Fire.

The Ascended Master Saint Germain represents Freedom to the Earth. He has become the Directive Intelligence for the next two thousand year cycle—the New Age, and in order to have the full action, the cosmic action of the Violet Flame He must be accepted; just as two thousand years ago, in order to have the grace over the Mosaic law, Jesus had to be accepted. Therefore the Ascended Master Saint Germain is presented first here; then Jesus Who was the Director of the previous two thousand year cycle and is now going into greater service;

then will follow the other Chohans in order of the rays; which will be followed by the various other Beings.

SAINT GERMAIN

Saint Germain's Cosmic Name is "Freedom". He is the Cosmic Father of the people of America.

Saint Germain's work for the freedom of mankind began in that civilization seventy thousand years ago; when a whole civilization could have been raised into the Ascension had they continued to give obedience instead of becoming rebellious (particularly in their feelings).

He with beloved Lady Master Nada have brought many civilizations to their height.

His work has been much more concerned with the human and physical realm than that of the Other Masters. He worked for two hundred years here in America before definite results began to manifest. This was brought about through the activity of the "I AM" Instruction; which important work has been the protection, purification and enlightenment of the people especially in America; and the purification of the Beings of the elements. Saint Germain took the responsibility for the students whether they gave obedience or not. When an Ascended Master does that and the necessary obedience is not given then He has to make up for that and give a balance to the great Law through application and Cosmic service, at inner levels.

Saint Germain was King of that great civilization seventy thousand years ago, where we find the Sahara Desert today. He possessed all the powers of a "Master" and could have made the Ascension as far as qualification goes. Some have wanted to know why He did not make the Ascension then when He had attained to such great heights. There is a very definite reason. He did not, so that he could embody again and again in order to hold a closer contact with the mankind of Earth. In this way He could accomplish things required for mankind's freedom in the future, since having a physical body gave Him a connection and authority which He would not have in the Ascended State. He retained continuity of consciousness from one embodiment to the next since that civilization seventy thousand years ago.

The term "Uncle Sam" really refers to Saint Germain Who instigated the establishment of our government. It was said that term comes from a former embodiment when He was Prophet Samuel, about eleventh century B. C.

Saint Germain was Joseph and with Mary prepared the way for Jesus. He was an Essene and knowing the mission of Jesus did some preparatory work among the disciples unbeknown to them, before they met Jesus. Saint Germain as Joseph was a very good example of the "Father" Jesus was to externalize through physical form and He was the ideal to Jesus in His childhood until He made the contact with Lord Maitreya. At the time of His passing (which was an easy one) He determined to give assistance to all to make their "passing easy"; for the animals as well as human beings.

Saint Germain was Saint Alban born in the third century in England presumably at the place of the present St. Alban. He was martyred about 303 during the persecution and later cannonized by the Church.

He was the Greek philosopher Proclus (411-485). This name became famous in after life. He composed hymns, embraced all religions and endeavored to unite all philosophies. He had a school in Athens, but he also traveled, studied and taught the various religions.

He was Merlin the magician of King Arthur's Court (in England, fifth and sixth centuries).

Another embodiment of his was as Roger Bacon (1211 or 14-1294) born at Ilchester, an English monk and philosopher, claimed by some to have been the greatest intellect which has arisen in England. He was a student of nature who was more physician than chemist, a scientist, and made many discoveries along this line in this lifetime as well as in many other embodiments, as he saw the need for the use of these things to benefit mankind. He studied at Oxford and then at Paris; there he received the degree of doctor of theology, then returned to Oxford. He became known as a father of science. He was known as the first naturalist by the Franciscan Order to which he belonged. He invented the spectacles, achromatic lenses and constructed the telescope; he did much experimental work and produced gunpowder which has been so greatly misused. He was one of the few astronomers of the time; he was responsible for the rectification of the Julian calendar. He was known as a magician and intensely interested in alchemy (transmutation) and in producing an elixir to prolong life. He wrote Opus Majus which was an encyclopedia of all sciences and for which he was persecuted.

Then as Christian Rosenkreutz of Germany in the fourteenth century he was sent to a monastery when only five years of age. He became a monk with real occult and spiritual knowledge. He journeyed through various countries and when only sixteen he came in contact with the wise men of Damcar in Arabia who received him as one they had long expected. He learned Arabic while there and translated a secret book into Latin, later he brought it to Europe. He went to Egypt after that and was welcomed by the Egyptian Brotherhood of the Great White Brotherhood (probably at Luxor) to which he had belonged in past lives. He went through the initiations there. Then Rosenkreutz returned to Germany and founded the Order of the "Rosy Cross", of which Rosicrucian is an off-spring. The Order consisted of only around thirty or forty members but it did form a school or focus for the secret mysteries and occult knowledge of the Great White Brotherhood in Europe which gave a direct connection with the Retreat.

It was said that Saint Germain was John Hunyadi who was a great Adept born in Transylvania, Hungary, in the early part of the fifteenth century (about 1387-1456).

Saint Germain as Christopher Columbus (1446?-1506) exhibited tremendous perseverance in that lifetime. History tells us he discovered America in 1492, but it is claimed that was not his first trip to this land. Columbus was a learned, cultured and talented person, a nobleman and not a beggar. He obtained much navigation information from the courts of Europe, particularly Spain and England. Some of Columbus' cryptic writings are still in existence which definitely bear out these facts. It was said from this time on Saint Germain was in embodiment continuously.

Paracelsus (1493-1541 Encyclopedia dates) * a Swiss chemist, physician and theosophist, was born near Zurich. He assumed the name of Aureolus Theophrastus Paracelsus. He learned from his father the rudiments of medicine, astrology and alchemy. He traveled over most parts of Europe, performed some healings and claimed to have discovered an elixir that would prolong life. He had an immense reputation in physics and surgery. His doctrine was that chemistry was to prepare medicines and not to make gold. It is claimed he was interested in that secret book translated by Christian Rosenkreutz.

There is mention made of Saint Germain having a short

---

* Here there may seem to be a discrepancy because dates stated according to history overlap. We were told by the Ascended Masters that dates were not always correct as given in history and the outer world, therefore they may not always correspond with certain information given by the Masters, Who can read the etheric records, but historians only form conclusions from heresay and outer means of acquiring information. In addition to the possibility of dates not being accurate there is an action of the inner law that a lifestream of great development, can manipulate such an event. The intricacy of that phase of the law cannot be given here.

embodiment before that of Francis Bacon. He was to have come to America as a boy, with De Soto and lived on the Wissahickon River in Pennsylvania.

Saint Germain's last embodiment was that of Francis Bacon (1561-1684) a philosopher and English writer. He was the son of Queen Elizabeth and rightful heir to the throne, this he was denied by the actions of his own mother. He wrote various books and articles under several different names, including plays by Shakespeare. A cipher code runs through these writings relating his real identity and the intrigue in court which prevented him from getting the right to the throne by which he had hoped to form a United States in Europe. Could this have been done there would have been no war there since. James I became king, instead. He misused government funds, but Francis Bacon, holding the accounts of England, took the blame for the wrong committed, to save the king and country.

Bacon used his plays and writings to influence the constituting of the English language of today. He supervised and edited the authorized version of the Bible (then being translated) which was directed by King James. Bacon's great work the Novum Organum (written in Latin) led the way to the development of modern inductive logic. This was the second instrument of thought, the first was Aristotle's Organon and the third is Ouspenski's Tertium Organum.

It is believed by some that he passed on in 1626. He let it appear that way and attended his own funeral in a woman's garb, but he did not leave the earth plane till May 1, 1684. He went from England to the Rakoczy mansion in Transylsvania and ascended on the Freedom Flame there into His eternal victory. The Goddess of Liberty was the first One to meet Him on the other side. He then went into the Great Silence for some time.

He was known as Prince Rakoczy of Transylvania and took many embodiments in that part of the world thereby drawing and establishing the Freedom Flame there. When he had passed the initiation whereby he was made the focus of the Freedom Flame to Earth he first embodied as a shepherd boy in Transylvania. He, then, for centuries, in each succeeding lifetime intensified and expanded that Flame.

The Master "R", known to us now as the Divine Director was his teacher and mentor and over-shadowed or enfolded him in His (Divine Director's) Cosmic Flame; as it was done in the case of Maitreya with the Master Jesus.

The Master Saint Germain appeared again in Europe and was known there during the time from 1710 to 1822, particularly. He appeared in His visible, tangible body in the various countries under various names. He kept close connections with influential people in these countries. He was known as Comte de Saint Germain in France, as the Wonderman in Germany, as Comte Bellamarre in Venice, as Prince Rakoczy at Dresden and by other names at different places. He was considered very wealthy and no one could determine from whence His wealth came.

It is not generally known that He was an Ascended Being at that time, which explains how He could so easily perform those super-human feats; and why He did not partake of food. Being Ascended He was therefore complete master over physical matter. He could appear in more than one place at the same time, he did not have to rely on outer world transportation and could precipitate whatever jewels, ornamentation and such like that He wished. His reason for exhibiting such wealth was for influential purposes, as that did impress them as nothing else would.

He called Himself Saint Germain (Sanctus Germanus which means holy brother). He would know what letters or newspapers contained without reading them. He could speak any language perfectly. He refused to accept any presents or benefits. He influenced the lives of many famous persons and people in governmental positions. He played a great part in the political world in America as well as in Europe during the eighteenth century. The original system of secret diplomacy was instigated by Him.

Saint Germain was personally known by the French kings, Louis XV and Louis XVI, and Queen Marie Antoinette. Had they heeded His advice it would have saved their and many others their lives during the French Revolution. Saint Germain told us in the latter nineteen-thirties that Marie Antoinette was at that time good at heart but did not withstand the influence at court; that she was in embodiment again in France and that He would see that she was brought in contact with this instruction.

Saint Germain was known by and worked with others in the French court, including Count Rochambeau. It is evident that the French expedition to America during the Revolutionary War in America and the appointment of General Rochambeau as its commander all came about through Saint Germain's influence.

He gave the elixir of life to several people which restored youth and beauty to them. He would write two different topics one with each hand, at the same time. He instructed and assisted Mesmer in his work, was known by Cagliostro, He exhibited alchemy to Casanova and assisted Charles of Hesse in the study of the secret science.

Saint Germain influenced the founding of many secret societies in various places, such as the Rosicrucians, Knights Templar, Knights of Light, the Illuminati and Masonry. These activities all coming under the ceremonial ray.

Napoleon knew Saint Germain intimately, Who taught and trained him and was the power behind him as long as he gave obedience. Saint Germain had to withdraw when Napoleon claimed the power as his own; and at that point is where his failure began. Saint Germain expected to make a United States of Europe through him, but again His efforts failed because of human weakness. Saint Germain was a friend of Frederick the Great and had a hand in placing Catharine the Great upon the throne of Russia. He was known by von Steuben and influenced him to come to America. General Washington, Lafayette and Franklin all knew Him, as did Lincoln later. They knew Him but they did not know He was an Ascended Being. He was the One (the unknown visitor) Who fired the patriots, Who swayed the Signers of the Declaration of Independence into signing the document; Whom they could not find afterwards, although the doors were locked and a man on guard. He was the inspiration and power behind the bringing forth of the Constitution of the United States as well as the Magna Carta of England. It was through His endeavors that George Washington was established as the first President of the United States of America.

His reputation in Europe was so great that even today there are people there who will bow at the mention of His name.

He was a power behind the building of trains, railroads, steamboats, airplanes and suspension bridges, most of which he had predicted as Roger Bacon.

He was also a friend of the writer Bulwer Lytton and evidently influential in his writings. The inspiration to produce the passion play every ten years by the people of Oberammergau came from Him.

Saint Germain was responsible for the culture in the Court of France and that of the Colonial Days. He was also responsible for the lovely Austrian music and much of the Venetian music. He inspired musicians such as Chopin, Tchaikowsky and especially Johann Strauss to write those Waltzes which are the music of His Retreat.

When He ceased working in Europe in the tangible form He said He would again be seen in eighty-five years which was around the time the Theosophical movement began.

Saint Germain was raised up and given the Ascension by Sanat Kumara.

Saint Germain became Chohan of the Seventh Ray (which office Kwan Yin was holding), around one hundred years after His Ascension. This was after His work at the Court of France and other parts of Europe, and after America's freedom, during which time He worked so much and closely in the physical realm. When He assumed the office of Chohan His service became Cosmic and He was no longer permitted to work in such close personal contact as before except with Napoleon.

Saint Germain endeavored at the court of France and in other parts of Europe to prove to the outer consciousness of the people through phenomena the inner powers and the power within themselves. He decided then that no longer would He attempt in that way to reach the hearts of mankind but He would employ another method. That He would use the means of instruction based on logic and common sense with radiation for the conviction of the instruction given; especially to people more interested in "works" than in phenomena.

Saint Germain was not so active in Theosophy, but instead He was building a momentum at inner levels and making preparation for the time when He would focus His ray in action in the outer again. This He did in the early nineteen-thirties through the I AM activity.

His work with mankind has been very great and through

all of that He has developed much patience with the people of Earth. We know little of what He went through to gain His eternal Freedom. It was far greater than what any of mankind have to encounter today. Therefore, He had the wisdom, strength and courage to bring forth the I AM Instruction and accomplished (in a few years) what none other was able to do.

Saint Germain was a priest in the Temple of Purification, the Temple of Violet Flame on Atlantis. He then received training at inner levels (both while in embodiment and in between embodiments), in divine alchemy in Archangel Zadkiel's' Temples over Cuba through the centuries after the sinking of Atlantis; until He qualified to become guardian of the Violet Flame and the Chohan of the Seventh Ray.

Saint Germain has worked for twelve thousand years hoping to bring forth a nation of Ascended Masters. He was able to precipitate hundreds of years before His Ascension. He said that He operated the law a long time before that "Great I AM Presence" was revealed to Him.

We were informed on December 21, 1937, that Saint Germain and Others of the Ascended Masters had walked the streets of some of our cities in Their tangible Bodies to give the needed protection through radiation. He said June 4, 1939, that He would move about in New York, Washington, D. C., Philadelphia and Cleveland once a week for the following six months.

Saint Germain had to wait a long time for the Goddess

of Justice (His Twin Ray) because She had ascended long before and had entered the Great Silence. She came forth in nineteen thirty-nine to assist Him in His work.

To secure dispensations beloved Saint Germain took the responsibility for the students, particularly, and for mankind.

Saint Germain was crowned May 1, 1954, and officially assumed the responsibilities as the Director for the new cycle of two thousand years on the Seventh Ray, and thus the initial pulsation flowed forth. This coronation gave Him the authority to increase an understanding of the presence and power of the Violet Ray and Flame as well as that of Freedom. Jesus held this position for the past two thousand years on the Sixth Ray; Saint Germain will now complete the work Jesus started.

Saint Germain also works as an Angel Deva, an Angel Deva of the Violet Flame, and has Legions of Angels under His direction. He is the Director of the Transmuting Violet Flame to the Earth.

His Retreat is the Rakoczy Mansion in Transylvania. He has a Focus in the Etheric City over the Sahara Desert, from which He works, directing light rays in His service to Earth. The Cave of Symbols is His Retreat in America.

An outstanding quality of His is enthusiasm for the Light.

He is about six feet one inch in height, has brown eyes and wavy brown hair. A fragrance He uses is that of violets. The electronic pattern of His lifestream is the Maltese Cross.

All great foundations start with one stone—that jeweled stone for the new age is the Ascended Master Saint Germain.

JESUS

It was said that Jesus was one of the guardians who came from Venus.

He was in embodiment at the time of Moses as Joshua. It is claimed by many that He was Apollonius of Tyana in the embodiment just before he embodied as Jesus. He then magnetized the healing rays which He utilized in His mission just before His Ascension. Previous to that He was a pilot on a merchant marine.

Jesus was prepared for many embodiments before that lifetime, in which He was to manifest the Christ and leave the example for mankind. He came into that embodiment without personal (karma) human creation, but He came into a mortal (physical) body created from physical substance with tendencies of race consciousness. A body of substance of the vibratory action of the physical world therefore not self-luminous in itself. It took on the luminosity at Transfiguration when His Christ Self expanded the light through Him to that extent. He had by applying this law and through the use of the Violet Flame and the Resurrection Flame, purified the substance of that physical body to the point where this could be done. This same action applies to the Lord Gautama and He worked His way through the psychic strata in Earth's atmosphere. Jesus started certain work for the purification of the Earth and the freedom of mankind then, which is only now being completed. He came at a point of great darkness and through His mission the currents were reversed.

The Christian dispensation was designed at inner levels. When the drama was shown on the cosmic screen, about thirty sixth ray individuals who had much development and mastery volunteered for the initiation of the public crucifixion. Jesus was the one chosen and then others were chosen who would come and be the guards, protectors, the mother, the father, the disciples and helpers.

The Three Wise Men with Jesus formed the square—the squaring of the circle.

Jesus as a small child first attended classes in the Temple at Karnak, Egypt. They were in Egypt a number of years before returning to the land of His birth.

Jesus also called Lord Maitreya "Father", Who was His Guru or Teacher, and Whom He recognized in His outer consciousness when yet a small boy. Their attunement and association grew and Their connection became closer and closer until They were as *one* in action. That is how the healing and so-called miracles were performed by Jesus.

He was in training in various Retreats, monasteries and such like during the period between the age of twelve and twenty-eight. He was in a monastery in Kashmir valley for five years, and there are scrolls preserved there which He wrote Himself.

Before Joseph passed on he informed Jesus that before He attained His majority He would be required to journey to India by foot to receive training from Joseph's Teacher and Master the Divine Director. Jesus made that journey soon after Joseph's passing.

He was in the Retreat for some length of time, when one day He received the mantram "I AM the Resurrection and the Life" from the Master. (A Master can convey an idea or message to his pupil on the inner and it need not necessarily be through the spoken word.) He had received no outer recognition from the Master although He knew perfectly well who Jesus was, His mission and of His coming. That statement was vital to Him—a key-phrase and He returned home, walked all the way, with that uppermost in His consciousness. The result of the use of that statement is a raising action. One thing definitely taught there, was that a decree had efficacy only when the truth affirmed was accepted and understood within the consciousness, in *feeling*.

He belonged to the Order of Zadkiel. He changed the quality of energy, He changed rough seas into peace, sickness into health, death into life.

Another statement Jesus gave which was not recorded, was "I AM the fulness of that great Light". When He said greater things than these shall ye do, He knew then that, as He went on into cosmic activity and would charge or enfold someone that was prepared, in His Flame of cosmic momentum they could then do even greater things than He did; also there would be greater opportunities, such as now. He had this instruction we have been given, and gave the teaching to approximately three thousand people. Spiritually He touched less than five hundred lifestreams in His lifetime. About five hundred witnessed His Ascension.

Jesus and Mary were at Luxor, Egypt, for about three years previous to Jesus' public ministry. There They both took the final intiation given at that Retreat. This initiation is to consciously suspend the breath from the body and then after a certain length of time animate the body again. This was done in preparation for Jesus' crucifixion.

Jesus did not suffer when He was on the cross because He had withdrawn His consciousness into His own Christ Self or Higher Mental Body; He kept just enough connection with the physical body to enable Him to speak those words, "Father how Thou hast glorified Me" (not forsaken me) which He spoke on the cross. When He had been taken off the cross His outer consciousness again entered the physical body. The three days He was in the tomb He completely purified that body by the use of light rays. When Archangel Gabriel rolled away the stone and He came forth that first Easter morning He had drawn the purified essence of the physical body into His own Christ Self and all else was consumed or transmuted. That was done through the action of the Resurrection Flame. There were only about twenty persons on Palm Sunday who were aware of the action and significance of that resurrection, to be; which was an externalization of the victory over death, and was not meant to portray the sorrows of crucifixion.

He was now the manifestation of the Christ Self and thus He walked and talked with His Mother Mary and some of His friends and disciples, for those forty days. The Christ Self is really consciousness and one must cultivate Its action through his thinking and feeling, until he develops the fullness of It.

Jesus had ascended into the Christ Self, that was one step, but He was not yet wholly ascended. The fortieth day when He walked to the top of Bethany Hill and entered the Heavens in blazing Light, that completed His Ascension. When Jesus ascended into the Electronic Body of His I AM Presence He poured forth an individualized flame around the heart of every lifestream embodied or dis-embodied, and will sustain it until each one is free in the Ascension.

Jesus, before His Ascension, also vowed (as Mary had) to assist those lifestreams who had lost their lives as babies by the order of King Herod. Jesus was permitted by the great Law to consume, transmute at inner levels at the time of His Ascension some karma for certain lifestreams. He could reach only some of those who were ready for spiritual enlightenment and who should have been reached during His ministry, but because of lack of transportation and communication facilities He was unable to reach them. Therefore, the Law permitted Him to give that assistance then. This has been misconstrued into the idea of vicarious atonement.

We were told the one on the cross to the right of Jesus did make the Ascension.

Jesus has appeared thousands of times since He ascended from Earth. He appeared twenty-one nights in succession and once five days later, to a noted artist who painted His portrait. When the painting was finished He ceased to appear.

One of Jesus' actions is the Central Sun magnet, which is drawing and directing currents of energy.

The fiat for the "Light as of a thousand suns" to descend if necessary, and transmute all human creation, was issued the third time August 22, 1937, by Jesus.

Jesus has been Chohan of the Sixth Ray since after His Ascension. January 1, 1956, He was raised to the position of World Teacher (along with Kuthumi), but still held connection with the Chohanship.

Jesus has golden hair and blue eyes. The music of "Joy to the World" would accompany Jesus' visitations after His Resurrection and often be heard before they were aware of His Presence.

MORYA

Morya came to Earth as a guardian from the planet Mercury. He is an Ascended Being now and Chohan of the First Ray, therefore an authority for its action to Earth. He represents the Will of God, gives assistance in all governments and stands by any one desirous of doing God's Will.

Most of His embodiments were masculine. He has been a king in many embodiments. He was Melchior, one of the Three Wise Men who found their way to the Christ Child. He could have had his Ascension then but refused it, in order to have a definite connection with the physical world which would not have been possible from the Ascended State, for that future date to bring forth Theosophy. Morya, Kuthumi and Djwal Kul endeavored through Theosophy to bring the understanding and truth of life and that there is no death; but mankind was not willing to give the necessary obedience which brought about spiritualism as a result. Theosophy acquainted seekers of Truth in the Western Hemisphere with the Masters. Here the Three worked together again, as They are also doing at present. Their Twin Rays or divine complements are in physical embodiment and rendering service to mankind under the guidance of the Great White Brotherhood.

Morya led three crusades. He was King Arthur of the fifth and sixth centuries. He took embodiment as Thomas More in 1478 in England; He is responsible for the poems by Sir Thomas Moore, the Irish poet. He purposely wrote poetry to soften his nature to get a better balance against the many embodiments of rulership.

Hercules was His Teacher. He also received training under the Lord Maha Chohan. He was a Rajput King of India. It was said that he retained that body for three hundred twenty-five years before he made the Ascension, around 1888.

He is Chief of the Council of the Great White Brotherhood at Darjeeling, India, and is in charge of the Retreat there. His disciplines are very strict.

He has dark brown hair and piercing brown eyes; He is around six feet six inches in height. The blue violet is His favorite flower. His keynote is "Panis Angelicus." His electronic pattern is the "cup", a chalice.

Morya was in our country in His tangible body in 1916, and in December 1937 He walked the streets of our cities to give the needed protection through radiation. He is One of the Beings Who direct the Cosmic action of the Rainbow Rays which were established May 24, 1938, from New York to Los Angeles and through the earth back to New York in a complete circle.

KUTHUMI

Kuthumi has been Chohan of the Second Ray and still held that office although He, with Jesus, had assumed responsibilities as World Teacher.

His action is illumination; His activity is education, giving understanding and wisdom through love. He is a Brother of the Golden Robe. He officiates at the Temple of Illumination or Wisdom over Kashmir.

Lord Maitreya was Kuthumi's teacher, but He was also trained under the Lord Maha Chohan and the Divine Director and was taught this exact instruction of the "I AM".

He was the Greek philosopher, Pythagoras (580-500? B. C.) in one embodiment. He settled in Southern Italy at Crotona between 540 and 530 B. C., where he made many important discoveries in various studies—mathematics, geometry, astronomy, and music. He determined that the world was round, that the planets produced music of the spheres and that the Real Self was immortal and came back into embodiment many times. He taught these doctrines at his school.

In another embodiment he was Balthazar, one of the Wise Men who followed the Star to the birth place of Jesus. He could have ascended then but like Morya did not, so as to have the closer physical connection to bring forth Theosophy in the future. Saint Francis of Assisi was another embodiment of his (1181 or 1182-1226). He was such a lover of nature that he would watch a certain phase for hours, or would stay a whole day with a flower to see it open into full bloom and perhaps watch it close again at night. He was one of the few who represented the heart of the nature kingdom. He was able to reach through the elemental kingdom and accelerate his consciousness to a point where he was of assistance in that realm. Birds and animals were drawn to him to be in his radiance which was about him; drawn by his constant attention and adoration to his Source. Saint Francis went out to preach in 1208. He founded the Order of Franciscan friars, the Order of St. Clara later, and then a third called Tertiaries. Some claim He was also the Pharaoh of Egypt, Thutmose III who erected the obelisk which is now in Central Park, New York. He built the Taj Mahal Hall (1630 to 1652) in another embodiment. He built it, one of the world's most beautiful buildings, for one he loved. It is said that now when marble is chipped off it replaces itself automatically.

Kuthumi was at Oxford University (1850), in his last embodiment and was instrumental in bringing forth Theosophy. He was from India. It was said he maintained that body for three hundred years; then went into a valley in the Himalayan Mountains and ascended from there, in about 1889.

He renders a certain definite service through music by playing His organ at His Focus at Shigatse in Tibet. He is one of the Ascended Masters Who walked the streets of our cities in December nineteen thirty-seven.

He is of a very gentle nature; and most gentle and patient in His presentation of instruction.

He has golden hair and blue eyes. His keynote is "Kashmiri Song (Pale Hands I Loved)".

PAUL—THE VENETIAN

Paul, The Venetian is known in this manner for the simple reason of distinction. He is the Chohan of the Third Ray, the Ray of love. He is the authority over the musical ray to Earth.

He was the artist Paolo Veronese, born in Italy, and well known for his paintings. One of his great paintings, perhaps the greatest, hangs now in the entrance hall of the Retreat in Southern France. This painting depicts the Holy Trinity.

He was in embodiment on Atlantis and went to Peru just before the Atlantean continent sank.

His interest is to nurture the undeveloped but latent talents in individuals by loving the Flame in their hearts.

He assists them through radiation to achieve beauty in all things and express perfection, and to fulfill their divine plan. He helps develop tolerance and love for one another. He carries the Adoration Flame to the consciousness of mankind as well as to Angels. One of His activities is the training of Elementals. He can be very firm too, in His discipline.

He attained the Ascension April 19, 1588, from the Retreat of the Liberty Flame in France. The Master Paul has golden hair and blue eyes. He is about six feet five inches in height. His keynote is "Love Song to Elsa" from Lohengrin (Wagner). His flower is the rose. His electronic pattern is the Three-fold Flame.

SERAPIS BEY

Serapis Bey is from the realm of Bey, hence the name, wherein is His dwelling place.

He is the great disciplinarian known through the centuries for the action of strict discipline. Real discipline is not stipulation over another which would thwart the innate progress, but instead it is a holding in check the human qualities so that the inner or *Real Self* can have expression. This is very essential to the attainment of the Ascension which is the culmination of all embodiments.

He came as a guardian to Earth's evolutions, and took physical embodiment as many did. It is said that He came from Venus.

His inner service is in the Fourth Sphere and He

works with the Christ Selves of the unascended life-streams there.

Serapis was the priest in the Ascension Temple on Atlantis before its sinking, to whom was delegated the task of taking a portion of the Ascension Flame to safety. He with forty of the Brotherhood sailed in a boat to Egypt, according to the directions they had been given. Just after their landing on the Nile River in the locality of Luxor they were aware of the sinking of Atlantis by the rumble and shaking of the Earth.

He established a Temple there for the Ascension Flame and has been the guardian of that Flame ever since. Some trusted Brother in physical embodiment would stand guard when he was at inner levels in between embodiments. Since the sinking of Atlantis around 12,000 years ago he has had nearly all embodiments in Egypt.

While in embodiment in Egypt as Akhenaton IV and Amenophis III he built the Temples at Thebes and at Karnak.

He was king Leonidas of Sparta and well known for the discipline at that time. He was in embodiment in Greece and had something to do with the creating of the Colossus at Rhodes at that time.

He was Phidias in one embodiment, an Athenian architect and sculptor. He brought forth the design of the Parthenon and supervised the building of it. According to one encyclopedia it was dedicated in 438 B. C.

He made the Ascension around 400 B. C. and after that He became Chohan of the Fourth Ray under which comes the action of the Ascension Flame. He is the Master in charge of the Brotherhood at Luxor, Egypt. He works with the Seraphim.

Serapis Bey has golden hair and His eyes are amber color. "Celeste Aida" is His keynote. His electronic pattern is a heart.

HILARION

Hilarion was a priest in the Temple of Truth on Atlantis and He with a group took the Flame of Truth and some documents to Greece. They arrived just shortly before the continent sank, thereby preserving that Flame for the Earth. He established the Focus of Truth there. Later the Oracles of Delphi were established and the initiates were directed by that Flame of Truth for hundreds of years. Great Truth came forth during that time. Then there came into the Temple some lifestreams not so pure and selfless but who yielded to other forces and could be bought. The people had faith in the Delphic Order because of the past and so fell prey to the wrong actions of the priests. It reached a point where the Masters had to withdraw and could no longer use it as a channel for giving forth wisdom. What is known about it in the outer world is from this phase of action of the Order.

He was Saul of Tarsus in Bible time and later known as Saint Paul, the Apostle. He was born of Jewish parents about the beginning of the Christian era, and was well versed in the Scriptures. His set beliefs as to how the

Messiah should come caused Him to miss seeing Jesus while on Earth. Soon after Jesus was Ascended He appeared to him while nearing Damascus on a journey undertaken for the purpose of searching out the disciples in that place and bringing them as prisoners to Jerusalem. In that visitation much of his arrogance and pride were consumed, he was convinced of the sinfulness of the course he was pursuing. His life was completely changed and he became a devout follower of Jesus' teachings.

He was blind after that for about three years due to karma, not only his own but the mass karma of lack of perception, for which he became a focus during that time of the change of cycles—the transference from the Fifth to the Sixth Ray. After a time he joined the colony of Mother Mary and the disciples. He suffered much remorse for having missed Jesus (while here) and for his actions against some of Jesus' followers.

He had received a commission from the Master Jesus to preach His teachings among the nations of the Earth. He was in retirement in Arabia for about three years before he started to carry out his new mission. It was due to him for the greater part, that the first distinctive mission to the Gentiles was undertaken. It is said that after his second arrest and trial he was martyred, and that was not later than the year 65 A. D.

It is said he was Iamblichus, born in Coele-Syria of an illustrious family. He studied in Rome, and later taught in Syria. Proclus mentions his works on Pythagorean philosophy.

Hilarion was born at Tabatha, near Gaza, Palestine (about 290-372; date from an encyclopedia). He was educated at Alexandria and is known as the reputed founder of Monasticism in Palestine. He lived as a hermit in the desert and after twenty years he had a great number of disciples and initiators under his spiritual direction. He departed from this earthly plane at a place among some almost inaccessible rocks and evidently ascended into His eternal Freedom. He was well known for his power of healing. He was commemorated by the Roman Church October twenty-first.

Hilarion is now Chohan of the Fifth Ray, the scientific ray. His hair is golden and His eyes are blue. "Onward Christian Soldiers" can be played to attune to Him.

He is particularly interested in assisting the agnostics, skeptics, atheists, spiritually disappointed and disillusioned ones, in inner realms as well as those in embodiment. He has great persuasive power and is very successful in instilling, again, faith in God into them. Hilarion and His Brotherhood also assist lifestreams at the time of passing and will take them to the Temple of Truth; They especially assist the non-believers in the here-after. He will assist anyone to know Truth who desires it.

People that believe in vicarious atonement find out when they have passed on, and are on the other side, that it is not as represented. It is such experiences that disillusions people who are sincerely seeking truth. When they are misled and become disappointed, that makes a record in the etheric body, and produces unbelief and skepticism, thus they become agnostics.

The Ascended Master Hilarion and the Brotherhood at Crete have offered to assist these people at inner levels. Another of Their services is to consecrate lifestreams of all seven rays who have a vocation.

Hilarion especially enjoys working on research in the medical profession. Healing is one of His main activities.

LADY MASTER NADA

The word "Nada" means "the voice of the silence", and also a receding of the personality into nothingness, giving way to the Christ Self.

Nada is a Messenger of Lord Meru and received training in His Retreat. She is of the Third Ray.

She has helped bring many civilizations to their height, even long before She was ascended. She worked with Saint Germain in that civilization seventy thousand years ago and in many since. She was also one who stood with Him when He first brought forth this instruction.

Nada, on Atlantis abided in the Temple which represented divine love, located where New Bedford, Massachusetts is now. They directed healing through love by use of light rays from that Temple to those who required it and could accept it, to anyone anywhere on Earth.

That Temple was patterned after a rose, each petal was a room. It still remains in the ethers even to this day.

Nada, in her last embodiment on Earth received training in developing divine love as a small child. She was the smallest and youngest of a large and wealthy family, who were all talented except she who seemed not to be. She felt her deficiency but one night a beautiful lady in pink appeared to her.

This Being taught her how to work with nature, the flowers and birds first, how to pour out love, a ray of light from her heart to them to which they would respond. This training of working with the rhythm of nature went on for several years. Nada noticed there would be a fragrance of roses and music whenever the lovely Being came.

Then one day the great Being informed her that Her name was Charity, and explained how she could render a service by pouring the love from her heart to the hearts of the ones in her family, while they slept, unbeknown to them. This way their talents were nourished and expanded and they became a great blessing to mankind, through music, art and poetry. Thus she became a "selfless one".

Her sisters married and she was home alone, then one day the Being Charity informed her that she was ready to enter into the activities of a Retreat. That she would have a visit by the Hierarch and that their association would cease. Then after a time Serapis Bey came and explained to her the requirements. That she would have to sever all connections with her family, enter a branch of the Retreat, there pass certain initiations before entering the Retreat at Luxor, where she could render service to those there by assisting them to release their own talents and fulfill their divine plan which was required before attaining the Ascension.

She went to this branch of the Retreat. The training there was particularly a harmonizing of various small groups into which she was placed and who found it very difficult to live together. She under-went some severe discipline. She had some very difficult times trying to maintain harmony during this phase of training and development, with frictions and the various human qualities that arose in their close association. She finally mastered them, and also learned that right within her own light, within and about her was everything that she required.

She was then admitted to the Retreat at Luxor where she rendered service for several centuries before she made the Ascension, around twenty-seven hundred years ago. She had assistance from the Divine Director in making the Ascension.

Her service is to amplify the good and the talents in others; pouring love to the Flame in their hearts, magnetizing and drawing forth the divine plan of that lifestream. She will render that same service to the students now.

Nada has a certain cosmic authority for the incoming age.

Healing is one of Her actions or services to mankind. She is One of those Who direct healing to the mankind of Earth. She said that many people had physical abnormalities in the functions of the body of which they were not aware. She offered to give assistance to individuals in this way as well as for bad habits, desires for wrong food, drink, smoking, et cetera, who would call to Her; the call gives Her permission to correct the conditions. She will also give assistance in legal matters.

She has a certain service in connection with precipitation for the student on the Path; and an action in directing the magnetic currents from the Central Sun.

We can call to Her to blanket the atmosphere with Her pink flame to prevent frost. When one is out in cold weather it is possible to be enfolded in Her pink Flame and therefore not feel the cold.

Nada is a Member of the Karmic Board and represents the Third Ray in that body. She has recently assumed the Chohanship for the Sixth Ray for the time being.

Nada is unusually small for an Ascended Being; She is around five feet two inches. She has golden hair and blue eyes. Her key-note is similar to "I Love You Only" from the "Chocolate Soldier". Her symbol is a pink rose.

ARCHANGELS

The Archangels come from the Central Sun. They are Beings Who serve in cosmic capacity. They direct legions of Angels. They have a work of Their own. The Archangels are the embodiment of some particular virtue.

The seven principal feelings required for mastery are represented by the Seven Archangels; of all activities the feelings are the most contagious. The Archangels represent the feelings of our nature. They represent and sustain the feeling, activities and qualities of the Creator for mankind's utilization and nourishment. They are the embodiment of qualified energy of certain qualities. Through Them flows the energies of the Seven Rays to the three kingdoms, angelic, human and elemental. The Seven Archangels and the Seven Archaii (Their Twin Rays) guard these three evolutions of all the planets of a system.

The Seven Archangels represented the seven great rays of creative power when mankind first came to Earth. Each One enfolded one of these rays, and was Chohan of that ray which formed the pattern to attain to, for some embodied lifestreams.

The Seven Archangels were the first to hold the offices of Chohans, representing the seven Rays; but have been practically forgotten since the sinking of Atlantis.

Faith, Hope and Charity have been forgotten by the people—the masses. They have worked together since the beginning of life upon this planet. They represent these three virtues to the Earth and these qualities are necessary for mankind to have, in order to fulfill their divine plan. These three qualities and activities are innate within every lifestream; they are anchored around the heart and help hold a balance which is necessary to attain mastery and the Ascension. The Cosmic Beings Faith, Hope and Charity have anchored a Flame of Their qualities around the heart of every human being, which radiate through the feelings.

Faith (blue), Hope (gold) and Charity (pink) represent an action of the Three-fold Flame to the Earth.

RAY	ARCHANGEL	ARCHAII
1	Michael	Faith
2	Jophiel	Constance
3	Chamuel	Charity
4	Gabriel	Hope
5	Raphael	Mary
6	Uriel	Donna Grace
7	Zadkiel	Amethyst

Archangel Michael is the Archangel of Protection and Faith, the Prince of the Angelic Hosts. He is the greater Lord of the Archangels, the Director of the Angelic Kingdom. He has the greatest legion of Angels of all the Archangels. He works in cosmic capacity although He is giving much assistance to individuals. He has been given recognition by some people throughout the centuries; more than any of the other Archangels. He offered to give protection to all taking embodiment on this planet and also all the other planets of this system, until all are ascended and have returned "Home".

He is also known as the Angel of Deliverance, because He frees lifestreams from human creation with His Sword of Blue Flame and whatever action of light is required. It was when the laggards came to Earth with their destructive thoughts and feelings and human creation began that He devised His Sword of Blue Flame as a means of service, which has been necessary through the ages.

He has protected the inner or spiritual light of individuals and sustained their faith since mankind began to draw shadows about them. This is a very great service He is rendering and He will continue until every lifestream is redeemed; until that time that each individual has gained mastery and is again perfect, free and ascended.

A particular activity of His is the cleansing of the atmosphere of Earth of the psychic substance, and individual lifestreams as well. He has worked in the atmosphere of Earth since the beginning of human creation, dissolving and transmuting much of it or mankind could not have survived. He has been serving in this capacity for twenty hours out of every twenty-four since nineteen thirty-nine. Now that has been increased to twenty-two hours out of every twenty-four. When He enters that realm He puts on full armor, helmet and all, to work with those destructive forces. He will remain until the Earth is free from them.

Archangel Michael came forth November 15, 1938, for the first time since His ministering in France through Joan of Arc; what He had undertaken to do then He will do in its fulness now. That night He started His service for America. He also released the dominion of the use of the Sword of Blue Flame into the students' hands.

Archangel Michael uses the Canadian Mounted Police as a focus in the outer; He also has a similar focus in southern Germany.

His Retreat is in the ethers in the Canadian Rockies.

He also has a Focus of Light in the etheric realm over Central Europe.

He has offered His shield of protection to the students. He has golden hair and blue eyes; and is usually dressed in blue with gold. His electronic pattern is a winged Cherubic head; the keynote is "The Wedding March" from Lohengrin (Wagner). His banner is a golden sun with the figures of the Seven Archangels on a blue background. September twenty-ninth is known as Michael's Day.

Faith is Archangel Michael's Twin Ray; They both work with Hercules.

Jophiel is the Archangel of Illumination. He represents the second ray and He was the first World Teacher for the Earth.

His service is to teach the outer consciousness the power of light within oneself, He stirs the feelings, through radiation of illumination into aspiration for spiritual things. One of His activities in His Temple is the training of the Angels. He holds a similar position to the Angelic kingdom now as the World Teacher does to mankind.

The Being **Constance** is His Twin Ray and represents the quality of constancy to those of Earth.

Chamuel is the Archangel of Adoration; He is the One on the third ray and the color is pink. His particular service for which we can call to Him, is to instill in us, and activate our feelings to joyously accept the God-Presence I AM ever-present in us.

The Being **Charity** and Chamuel are Twin Rays. She

represents the quality and activity of charity to Earth.

Charity is the quality of forgiving love. Her Flame anchored (around the heart) within the individual can consume the wrong and hard feelings by forgiving love which is necessary, as real forgiveness is a feeling *not* just an intellectual thing. Her Flame of charity, when there is enough of it allowed to flow through, prevents the action of discord. The color of the Flame is pink. Charity represents the inner love—the expression of inner love. Charity is the expression of gratitude and thanksgiving. She is the embodiment of love for life.

Both Chamuel and Charity have golden hair and violet eyes.

Gabriel the Archangel of Resurrection is of the fourth ray, He dwells in the Fourth Realm or Sphere and works with Serapis there. He knows well the divine plan of each lifestream belonging to Earth as He is well acquainted with the Christ Selves. He came to Earth and has stayed for the purpose of holding the Divine Concept for every individual and his divine plan as well as for the Earth.

His service is to induce the feeling into the outer consciousness of the reality of each one's own Christ Self and becoming one with It; of resurrecting the latent powers within the lifestream.

Gabriel promised Mary before She took embodiment as the Mother of Jesus that He would bring to Her outer consciousness at the right time the mission She was to fulfill, and then enabled Her to see Jesus' I AM Presence. This enabled Her to hold that concept of perfection, that visualization for Him all through His lifetime.

He also assisted in the Resurrection of Jesus' body. He was the Angel Who rolled away the stone from the tomb on that first Easter morn.

He has golden hair; His keynote is "Intermezzo" from the opera Cavalleria Rusticana.

The Being **Hope** and Gabriel are Twin Rays.

Hope is eternal, it is ever present even in the darkest hours of any one's life. The quality hope is that one may proceed into greater light. There is deep within each one a ray of hope of some kind. That is because the Cosmic Being Hope has implanted a ray of Her quality within each lifestream and through that She can intensify the feeling of hope at any moment. That way She assists the Christ Self to fulfill the divine plan. Her service is to instill and sustain hope and enthusiasm in everyone. Hope gives a feeling of expectancy and buoyancy. She is the Spirit of Resurrection. She and Gabriel work from the Resurrection Temple.

Raphael is the Archangel of Consecration and Concentration. His is the office of dedication. He gives God-assistance to lifestreams who have dedicated themselves to service to mankind and to world missions. His action is that of concentration.

His keynote is "Whispering Hope" (hymn).

His Twin Ray is **Mary**, Mother of Jesus.

Uriel the Archangel of Ministration offered to minister to all who embody here and all life on Earth, to bring healing and peace to the body, feelings and mind. Each one's Ministering Angel does likewise. Uriel ministers to all who call to God for healing or whatever it may be. He has great Legions of Angels Who assist to carry out His service.

The Twin Ray of Uriel is **Donna Grace** Who embodies the virtue of grace, which is a feeling. It is a *feeling* not only a gesture. Donna Grace is the representative of grace in the Angelic kingdom in a similar manner as Mary represents grace to mankind.

Zadkiel the Archangel of Invocation is of the Seventh Ray. He guards the powers of invocation. This is His service to life. His Focus is in the etheric realm over Cuba. His color is royal purple and He uses the amethyst jewel which is a condensation of the violet ray.

His Twin Ray's name is **Amethyst.** She is the Intelligence within the Transmuting Violet Flame.

THE SEVEN ELOHIM

The Elohim direct the one creative power (force). They direct and operate the creative energy of a universe. The Seven Elohim are the builders of this system.

The energy used on a planet and its mankind comes from the Central Sun through the Sun of the system and then through the Seven Elohim where it is diversified. Thus are the seven rays to a planet directed through the Seven Elohim. The seven rays of light are directed by Seven Great Beings known as the Elohim. They are great Cosmic Beings from out the Central Sun. The

Seven Elohim are the conductors of the seven activities of the Godhead through the seven rays. They represent the seven attributes of form to the planets.

The Seven Elohim represent the mental activities and qualities (of the Creator). A tiny Flame from each of Their lifestreams is anchored in the forehead of every individual embodying on Earth. They give of Their faculties and consciousness to every lifestream through the seven-fold Flame anchored in the forehead; this comes through the intellect to assist in holding a balance and fulfilling the divine plan in the outer world.

Their rays are also directed through the Archangels.

Elohim were elementals and became Elohim, then They can become Cosmic Silent Watchers if They wish.

The Seven ELOHIM and Their TWIN RAYS or Divine Complements:

RAY	MASCULINE ASPECT	FEMININE ASPECT
1	Hercules	Amazon
2	Cassiopea	Minerva
3	Orion	Angelica
4	Eloah of Purity—Clair	Astrea
5	Vista—Cyclopia	Crystal
6	Eloah of Peace—Tranquility	Pacifica
7	Arcturus	Diana

Hercules is Eloah of Power. He is the Eloah on the First Ray. He represents God's Will, His is the action to do the Will of God. He is guardian of the energy released and used on the planets.

Hercules summoned the other Elohim to carry out Helios' and Vesta's plan for the creation of this system.

He is known for power and strength, but His power is love, not His form or body, although He is nearly fourteen feet in height.

One can call to Him for courage and strength. Power is concentrated energy (force, of action). His predominant color is blue.

Amazon is also of large stature and very powerful.

Cassiopea is the Eloah of Wisdom. He directs and governs the actions of perception, comprehension, illumination, understanding and the power of (concentrated) attention. Cassiopea is Eloah of the Second Ray. His predominant color is yellow-gold.

Minerva is also known as the Goddess of Wisdom.

Orion is Eloah of Divine Love. There are several Beings referred to as Orion; the Eloah of the Third Ray is One. He governs the activity of Divine Love, Cosmic Love. Within this love is the cohesive power that draws and holds form together. The predominant color is pink.

Angelica, as the name implies, carries the quality of extreme love.

Eloah of Purity also known as Clair, represents Cosmic Purity to this system, which maintains perfection. He is the Eloah of the Fourth Ray.

He will release the Cosmic Blue Lightning of Divine Love at one's call into any condition or through the inner bodies to shatter hard or accumulated substance; it can then more readily be transmuted. The Blue Lightning explodes the center of destructive focuses (vortices), releasing the life essence, this releases the elementals' vow to remain and obey destructive forces. That life essence can then return to the Sun for re-polarization. This is how epidemics can be stopped.

The color is predominantly white or crystal.

Eloah of Purity's and Astrea's services are the purifying of the atmosphere of Earth and mankind's inner bodies in general as well as individually. Their service in this solar system is the holding of the divine (perfect) concept for the Earth and all thereon.

Astrea is a great Cosmic Being Who came forth into definite action in nineteen thirty-seven. This particular action is the consuming and transmuting of the psychic or astral substance in the atmosphere as well as those qualities in the individual lifestreams, when the call is made. The Circle and Sword of Blue Flame are used for this action. This great Being has been instrumental in the tremendous task of removing the black magicians, the great number of disembodied individuals that were earth bound, and much of the psychic substance, the destructive forces and vortices.

When Astrea first came forth this Being was referred to as masculine. Then some years later it was given out that Astrea was the Twin Ray of the Eloah of Purity and therefore taken to be the feminine aspect instead of masculine. However, since They can operate or work from either the masculine or feminine aspect it can readily be seen that because of the nature of the task undertaken at that time the masculine aspect may have been used.

Astrea rendered a great service for Seattle, Washington, September 22, 1938, during the class there. It was stated July 16, 1939, that Astrea had decided to come forth and move through the atmosphere of Earth; later it was said She would continue at least until the end of January 1940. She has constantly answered the calls of the students since that time.

Astrea is from the fourth sphere.

Vista is known to some as Cyclopea; but is known as Vista in the inner realms. He is the **Eloah of** Concentration and Consecration; He is also **Eloah of Music.** He is **Eloah of** the Fifth Ray. He governs the All-Seeing Eye of God to this system, all activity of sight, hearing and speech; healing is one of His actions also. His action is concentration, consecration and the action of seeing vistas ahead.

Vista works from the Emerald and Crystal Temples. The predominant color is green.

Previous to the starting of this instruction coming forth in 1930-1931 this great Cosmic Being came forth only once every hundred years. Since then He has come to the Teton Conclaves every six months where He would release great blue balls of fire into the atmosphere and direct currents of energy along with the light rays focused through the Eye in the wall at the north end of the Sanctuary in the Teton Retreat, for clarifying purposes.

He is One of the Members of the Karmic Board, He represents the fifth ray on that Board.

A great Master was placed over Canada December 5, 1938, later it was given out that that was Cyclopea—Vista.

Crystal has offered to assist in the clarification of the inner bodies; healing comes under Her action also.

Eloah of Peace is also known as Tranquility; He is the Eloah of the Sixth Ray. Peace is His special quality and activity. He represents the concentrated action of peace to this system. Peace is the sustaining power of manifest form, and is so essential. Ministration is His action also. The color is deep pink and gold.

Pacifica is the embodiment of very great peace as the name implies.

Arcturus is the Eloah of Freedom; Eloah of the Violet Flame, and of Mercy. He is the Eloah of the Seventh Ray. His action is that of invocation and the rhythm of application. He directs the Violet Ray to Earth.

He is the great Being in this solar system Who answers the heart call for Freedom, when intense and sincere, freedom from any limitation or imperfection. He will assist one to release qualities, powers and activities of life which are within each one's lifestream.

He is the One that connects the flames in the heart, throat and forehead of a disciple at a certain point on the Path.

When His ray lit the lights (rang a bell and started

a flame) at the opening of the Century of Progress Exposition in Chicago in nineteen thirty-three, He started into action the expansion of His Flame in America. The Star Arcturus is His Focus or Home.

He was the One to issue the fiat the second time (August 19, 1934), that that light as of a thousand suns shall descend if necessary for the protection of America.

Diana's service is in the intensification of this Flame of purification; to expand the light from within and release and transmute the dense substance lodged around the electrons, the pure light, in the four lower bodies. This raises the vibratory action and restores the bodies and brings them back into tune with their own keynote and fragrance.

HELIOS AND VESTA
Sun God and Goddess

Helios and Vesta are Twin Rays. They are the self-conscious Beings which are the focal point of the Sun of our system. They and Their Causal Bodies, radiation and activities composes the Sun. They represent the Godhead to this solar system. They are the authority for this system. This planet and whole system was first designed from Their light, Their minds' thought and hearts' love. The Sun God and Sun Goddess are not the Sun, Themselves; They are individual Cosmic Beings and are the focus of or for the Sun. A crude illustration might be one's home or business. The home is not the parents of a family but it is the actions and substance drawn together by them and under their direction which forms a focus creating a home, or business. The same principle applies to the expression of the Earth being the body of the Being Virgo.

All life, all that is manifest in or on Earth or in its atmosphere and even in this whole system, comes through the Sun of the system, which has been drawn from the Source the Central Sun, and qualified, therefore under the direction of Helios and Vesta. All the Ascended Masters and Cosmic Beings do for the planet and its people is done in cooperation with the Sun God and Goddess.

It is the fire element from the Sun that is the life, light and sustaining power of a system of worlds. Helios' and Vesta's Cosmic service is the outpouring of the fire element to this system. Their auras consist of all the virtues and activities of These Beings, which form the nature of the Godhead and the Cosmic Holy Spirit for the solar system. Their Causal Bodies which have been created by Their drawing and qualifying energy, are sustained by Their love. Their combined Causal Bodies form the spheres of this universe.

There is evolution or expansion continually going on in the Sun. It functions similar to a planet only at a much higher or greater degree and expanse.

Helios and Vesta are the God-Parents of the individual Flames of the lifestreams (mankind) of Earth and the other planets of this solar system, those who originally came forth to evolve on these planets. They are as foster parents to the guardians who came from other systems to assist mankind; their real God-Parents being the Sun God and Goddess of the system from whence they came. This is also the action for the laggards on Earth who came from other systems.

Each Sun is endowed with two particular qualities which are the predominant qualities of the Sun God and Goddess. The one of Helios' is Illumination and Vesta's is Truth.

Vesta was the first Goddess of Truth to the Earth.

Helios blesses every lifestream through music. Salamanders are created by Him.

THE SILENT WATCHERS

The term Silent Watcher is applied to many and various types of Beings. Their service is to stand over and guard any action, or that of a group. There is a Silent Watcher usually an Angel Deva, over every group, city, locality, state, country and planet.

There is a Silent Watcher for each planet; and there is a greater One for the system, this Cosmic Silent Watcher is the first Being working under or out from the Sun.

The Silent Watcher of an individual is his own Christ Self.

A Silent Watcher holds within the consciousness the pattern to be outpictured.

The Silent Watcher of the planet Earth holds the pattern and whole plan in the consciousness for the Earth and all her evolutions from the beginning to completion. She is the smallest of the Planetary Silent Watchers of this system. Her name is Immaculata. She usually wears robes of blue.

The Planetary Silent Watcher gives the divine plan of the planet to the Lord of the World. The power of that Being is fearlessness. She will give amplification to music.

The Causal Body of the Planetary Silent Watcher forms the spheres around the planet.

THE HALLS OF KARMA—THE KARMIC BOARD

There is existent in the etheric realm a large white building known as the Halls of Karma or "Judgment Halls", wherein the Lords of Karma officiate in regard to lifestreams, individually and collectively in connection with their imperfect karma and their future progress. There, individuals after passing (through so-called death) are assigned in mercy and love to school rooms or their proper place where they dwell until they re-embody. All this comes under the jurisdiction of the Karmic Board.

The Karmic Board was established when the need arose after mankind began to create the shadows. It is an instrument of mercy instead of judgment. It consists of Seven Great Beings, officiating in Cosmic capacity. These Lords of Karma are Cosmic Beings of tremendous Divine Love. They are completely impersonal and impassionate in Their judgment, always acting for the good of all. They are interested in the greatest development and the fulfillment of the divine plan for each individual as well as all life.

Their action is one of mercy to individuals as well as

to groups and nations. They have taken on the responsibility to see that all energies are purified and redeemed. They endeavor to work out ways and means to mitigate the imperfect karma created through the misuse of primal life. It is not a hard and cruel judgment but that which will be the best for the development and progress of the lifestream, and at no time an act of condemnation. Their service is indeed a thankless one from the mankind of Earth.

One action of the Karmic Board is to designate which individuals are to embody. It has been Their responsibility to select and direct which lifestreams would be allowed to take embodiment. This is done according to individual karma of imperfection, in order to keep sufficient balance with those lifestreams passing on or leaving the Earth, so as not to cause too great a weight; also as to lifestreams who have offered to render service, They consider their good karma, the accumulated good. They in mercy regulate the bad karma of all mankind. They in mercy regulate the return of the individual human creation so that it is not greater than he can handle, to judge how much the individual could stand and give opportunity for the redemption of a certain amount in a lifetime, and thus make progress. Its judgment is not in a sense of punishment, but what can be the greatest good for the lifestream.

The Lords of Karma give each one the greatest opportunity possible according to his own light and the karma created by him, it is this decision that is referred to as "judgment". This has caused fear in some people and they dread the Halls of Karma. That is because every experience they have had before those great Lords (which is the judgment day) is recorded in their etheric bodies. Many of those days may have been remorseful when the individual saw what was left undone and "what could have been" instead.

The Seven Members of the Karmic Board at present, and the Ray Each represents are:

RAY	LORD OF KARMA
1	Divine Director
2	Goddess of Liberty
3	Nada
4	Pallas Athena
5	Vista (Cyclopea)
6	Kwan Yin
7	Portia—Goddess of Justice and Opportunity

The Karmic Board convenes twice yearly—around the first of January and the first of July, at the Grand Teton Retreat. They are seated according to the rays They represent, rays one to seven from left to right, but as different Ones take the office of Spokesman, then that One takes the center chair, with Three on either side.

The Karmic Board was established with the Goddess of Liberty as Spokesman, which office She held for many thousands of years. It is only within recent years that the various Ones have been Spokesman. A few years ago at a ceremony at inner levels, the Goddess of Liberty transferred the authority to Kwan Yin. The authority of

Spokesman was transferred June 27, 1954, from Kwan Yin to the Goddess of Justice for the next two thousand years in honor of Saint Germain's position as presiding Master for this new cycle. However, one of the others on the Board does act as Spokesman on certain occasions or for a certain period of time.

The Karmic Board has been the supreme authority for mankind through the centuries; Their decisions were final. They represent the Cosmic Law which governs the affairs and progress of the Earth and all life on it. Now, since Helios and Vesta Who represent the heart of this system, have joined the Cosmic Council They are the superior authority. This has enabled greater lee-way to be given in a spiritual way.

The Karmic Board presides over the half-yearly Councils which consist of Ascended Masters, Cosmic Beings, Angels and now some unascended beings in their inner bodies, who are interested in formulating plans and petitions for the betterment of the race and the Earth, and the establishment of permanent perfection. The Karmic Board passes on petitions and gives opportunity to the Hierarchy and those unascended in the outer world, working with Them, to further God's Will and the divine plan.

The Members of the Karmic Board wear seven-pointed crowns.

THE LORD OF THE WORLD

The Lord of the World is the authority and highest governing Being of the Spiritual Hierarchy of a planet and its evolutions.

He gets the divine plan for the planet's progress and its evolutions from the Planetary Silent Watcher. He becomes the Illuminating Presence and guardian for all life on the planet. He and the Lords of Karma for the Earth work together.

There have been several Lords of the World for the Earth.

SANAT KUMARA

Sanat Kumara took the place of Shri Magra the previous Lord of the World, and has held this position for a very long time.

The great Being Sanat Kumara is referred to in the Bible as the "Ancient of Days", by some He is known as the "Lord of the World", also as the Lord of the Flame, He and the other Kumaras being called the "Lords of the Flame." Kumara is a title which means Ruler or Prince. The Seven Kumaras (The Lords of the Flame from Venus) are Messengers of the Seven Elohim from the Central Sun, to Venus.

Sanat Kumara came to Earth and has abided in the atmosphere, in what is now the Etheric City over the Gobi Desert. Three Kumaras have assisted Him. He never took physical embodiment on Earth as He was an Ascended Being and worked in cosmic capacities before He came to assist the Earth.

Sanat Kumara came ages ago to give assistance to the Earth when it would have been dissolved otherwise. He offered of His own free will to supply the light required to sustain her and keep her place in the system until enough of mankind could be raised to a point where they could carry the responsibility of emitting sufficient light.

He drew forth the Three-fold Flame at Shamballa (an action from Venus) and a small thread of light from It tied into the hearts of all who were embodying on Earth (whether in or out of embodiment); this gave them a new impetus and new life. He has nourished, sustained and guarded the Flame in the hearts of the mankind of Earth. It is only because of this assistance from Him that we have been sustained here through the centuries, otherwise the Christ Selves (Higher Mental Bodies) would have withdrawn completely which would have resulted in the second death, as it is called. Thus have the other actions of the Sacred Fire been sustained also.

He gave the Sacred Fire in wood during a certain period. The people came to the ceremony once a year and took a piece of the wood home with them; He sustained the Fire which kept the atmosphere clear and enabled them to hold contact with their own Presence.

Sanat Kumara has been the head of the Hierarchy and the human kingdom although mankind had completely forgotten Him. Even His name was unknown to mankind for many centuries. Now when people first come in contact with His name they usually feel a sense of happiness come over them. This is because of His connection with their lifestreams through radiation during the past. These last centuries the only place Sanat Kumara gave direct radiance on Earth was in India at the Wesak Festival through the Lord Maha Chohan.

His predominant qualities are love, patience, illumination, as well as balance. Being Venus is His Twin Ray.

Redemption of mankind was expected and should have taken place long before this, yet His love and patience has never wavered. Even now when the cosmic law says He must be released within a certain period of time (in fourteen years or so), He still is willing to stay longer if mankind is not prepared by that time.

Sanat Kumara was given His freedom on January 1, 1956, from exile on Earth. However, He took the position of Regent for the time being, still assisting Earth while making adjustments and serving on Venus, His Home. He is still assisting Earth and her people to hold a balance during this process of change, physically and chemically as well as on the inner.

LORD GAUTAMA

Lord Gautama and Lord Maitreya were the first lifestreams of unascended mankind who responded to the love of Sanat Kumara for volunteers after He had come to Earth and taken her under His wing, so to speak.

The positions of the Hierarchy had always been held by Ascended Beings from other planets and not by Beings who gained their attainment on Earth. The Being holding the position of Buddha had asked to be released so that He might go on with His own evolution. It was required that one from the guardians of Earth be developed to embody the nature of God to qualify for the position of Buddha. Lord Gautama and Lord Maitreya both offered to make the endeavor.

They then went through many embodiments on Earth and many times were in embodiment at the same time, both having similar training. This was done not in competition but in loving service and in between embodiments in the inner realms They would compare their experiences and progress.

Lord Gautama knew great light and illumination on Lemuria. It was said that He was the first of the twenty-nine Zarathustras; that He was Hermes of ancient Egypt, known as "Father of All Wisdom", and Orpheus of Greece.

He was in embodiment as Prince Siddartha Gautama the son of a King in India. He was born May 8th (563-483 B. C., according to a dictionary). He came into that embodiment without personal karma. He grew up protected within the palace and did not know of mankind's distresses, disease and death. He married Princess Yasodhra (His Twin Ray). A son (Rohula) was born to them, and while he was yet a baby, Siddartha left home and family, renouncing his ascension to the throne, to go out in search of Truth. He became an ascetic and after six years he entered into deep meditation—contemplation, during which time He was confronted with many human qualities and temptations.

He raised Himself in consciousness, through application consciously passing through the various spheres (strata of consciousness) and into the great eternal light; thus becoming master over vibration, energy and substance. He went further than some, seeking the ultimate, though there really is none, as there are ever greater heights to attain, no matter how far one may go. He went on until He became the fulness of love.

He attained illumination and was transfigured, hence the term "The Enlightened One" has been attributed to Him. He gained the qualifications of a Buddha and was known as Gautama Buddha or just Buddha. He made this attainment at inner levels, in seven years, while His physical body sat under the bo-tree at Gaya, and was taken care of by some chelas of His. He then came back, consciously descended and again functioned through his physical body, sacrificing His inner attainment. This renunciation and the centuries of training is what is referred to as the Great Sacrifice. He re-animated His physical body which had become greatly emaciated, and again functioned among mankind, expressing the nature of divinity. Thus He served in the world of form for some forty-five years, walking the land of India, teaching the Truth by word, radiation and example, stressing the Path of the Middle Way. He fulfilled a great mission.

Lord Gautama attained while in physical embodiment to the point where His aura was so charged with divine qualities that upon touching a lifestream it would cause that one to experience an exaltation of consciousness. He magnetized great currents of energy in that lifetime as well as in previous embodiments which still radiate their blessings to mankind.

Lord Gautama at one time served as Chohan of the Seventh Ray.

BUDDHA

Buddha is a certain attainment and qualification as well as a particular position in the Spiritual Hierarchy. Buddha is a second ray activity.

There have been several Beings Who held the position of Buddha for Earth. The next step from here is Lord of the World.

The activity and service of a Buddha is to step down the high spiritual vibrations and radiate them to nourish, expand and sustain the light in all beings during their development on the planet. He is to radiate God's love to a planet and its evolutions; to draw and hold the spiritual nourishment around a planet for all evolving life-streams on that planet both while in and out of embodiment, sustaining them spiritually and developing their inner or God natures especially the emotional bodies. He guards and sustains the flame of the least developed soul, so that it will not go out. A Buddha's work is through radiation, by radiating.

Lord Gautama was the first from the humanity of Earth to hold the position of Buddha, the previous ones having come from other planets. Gautama Buddha reached that attainment ahead of Lord Maitreya and so became the

Buddha while Lord Maitreya was placed in the next position—the World Teacher.

Lord Gautama served at inner levels since His Ascension, only appearing and rendering service at the Wesak Festival in His Luminous Presence.

He returned to Earth in His Ascended Body for the first time on February 23, 1953. He stayed and has worked in the atmosphere of Earth since that time.

He became Lord of the World when Sanat Kumara was given His freedom on January 1, 1956. He was a guardian who took physical embodiment on Earth many times and this has given Him a specific qualification for Lord of the World at this particular time, because He had experienced the discordant conditions of the humanity of Earth. He was prepared and ready to assume this high office when the time came that Sanat Kumara could be released.

Lord Gautama's particular quality is balance and He will give assistance in the balancing of the four lower bodies. He came from Venus. His Electronic pattern is a lotus; He has golden hair and blue eyes. He made the Ascension on May the eighth, on the anniversary of His Enlightenment, which was also His birthday. The music "Song of India" is used for His keynote.

LORD MAITREYA

Lord Maitreya means Lord of Love.

Lord Maitreya has held the office of World Teacher in the Hierarchy; He assumed the office of the Buddha on January 1, 1956, but still holds a connection and a certain action with His former position. The Master Kuthumi and Jesus have jointly assumed this office.

Maitreya has been known through the centuries as the Great Initiator, under the old or occult law. He represented the Cosmic Christ to mankind of Earth which was a similar action to the individual as that of his own Christ Self. This was necessary because mankind had gotten into so much discord and density that their own Christ Selves no longer responded or acted in that respect or degree in the outer self. Therefore, the Great Initiator represented and acted for the Christ Self of an individual on the Path to a certain extent.

That is why it was necessary for Jesus' manifestation of the Christ in/through a physical body. This plan was so designed beforehand, as being the best way to convince or/and leave an example of the Christ Action for the consciousness of mankind who were not comprehending beyond the world of form.

Lord Maitreya was not an incarnation of Jesus (They are two separate lifestreams). He enfolded Jesus in His Cosmic Flame and thereby manifested the Christ Consciousness through Jesus' form. He likewise enfolded Saint Patrick, another individual in a physical body.

Now that the Cosmic Light is flooding the Earth and its atmosphere It (the Cosmic Light) acts as the Initiator to mankind. There is more and more expansion of the individual's own light as the Cosmic Light increases.

Finally when mankind and the Earth have been cleansed of all impurities the inner bodies (emotional, mental and etheric) and the atmosphere of Earth will become all light, and the individual's own Christ Self will again take full command of the outer self.

WORLD TEACHER

The World Teacher works under the Lord of the World on the second ray. He is the educator, developing the conscious mind—the indwelling consciousness in connection with the radiation from the Buddha. His service is to bring understanding to the conscious mind and develop the Christ activity in each individual.

The natural length of time for a Being serving in this capacity is for the duration of a fourteen thousand year cycle. Each of the World Teachers of the first, second and third root race has gone on with His race.

The World Teacher gets the divine plan from the Silent Watcher and then designs the type of spiritual teaching which is best to send forth into the world for that particular cycle. He in cooperation with the Chohan of that (two thousand year) cycle work out a plan for the presentation of the teaching and radiation for the spiritual development of the people during that cycle.

The World Teacher is a teacher of teachers.

Lord Maitreya came to Earth from Venus as a guardian. He knew His greatest light in embodiment in the East with Lord Himalaya. He has a Focus in the

Himalayan Mountains. He has violet eyes and golden hair. His keynote is "Ah! Sweet Mystery of Life," by Victor Herbert. He usually wears a white robe.

Lord Maitreya anchored a ray from the realms of light into New York City and one into Los Angeles on October 8, 1937, to hold a balance in America on the east and west coasts of the United States for the incoming age.

He now holds the position as the Buddha; He carries out the activities of ceremonies to relieve Lord Gautama as much as possible, since His inclination is not along that line.

MAHA CHOHAN

There is the office of Maha Chohan in the Spiritual Hierarchy as well as the Individual Being. Lord Maha means Great Lord. He is Lord over the Chohans.

Maha Chohan is a third ray activity. It has been the office through which the Godhead worked on the rays from the third to the seventh. However, this action changed recently (a few years ago), and the first and second rays now also come under the Maha Chohan.

A Being must have developed and embodied all the divine virtues and have mastered all of the seven rays before He qualified to be a Maha Chohan.

A Maha Chohan represents the Holy Spirit (which consists of all the divine qualities of the Godhead) to a planet. The Holy Spirit represents action and light and vitalizes whatever ray is in action. The Maha Chohan is the director of the activity of the Holy Spirit for the

Earth which assists the development of the divine feelings in mankind.

Holy Ghost really means Holy Spirit (the word ghost refers to a shadowy, ephemeral thing). The Holy Spirit is the consciousness of the Lord Maha Chohan, His powers, qualities and activities, His Cosmic Flame.

It was He that enfolded Jesus in His Cosmic Flame at the time of the baptism by John the Baptist, endowing Jesus with His powers. It was His action when the Holy Spirit descended upon the Disciples ten days after Jesus' Ascension; that was the radiation from the Lord Maha Chohan. He enfolded them in His Cosmic Flame which gave to them the assurance, courage, strength and power to carry on the teaching and works of Jesus. "The Comforter" referred to is the Lord Maha Chohan.

The first Maha Chohan Who came with the first root race in the beginning established the Flame of the Holy Spirit and the Comfort Flame here on Earth. The three Maha Chohans of the first root races have each gone on with Their race. Feminine Beings have held this position.

The Maha Chohan is at the head of the Elemental kingdom; and is the authority over manifestations in nature. He draws and supplies the energy used in all nature and by mankind. He is the magnet to draw that power from the Sun.

He directs the various forms of culture and civilizations through the minds of embodied individuals so as to unfold and develop according to the divine plan.

The Maha Chohan is the One Who gives the first breath

to every new born child; He also takes the last breath of every individual as he passes on.

The Lord Maha Chohan has not had personal contact with chelas (students) through the ages, as He does now.

It is said that the great Ascended Being Who is now the Lord Maha Chohan was embodied as Homer, the blind poet. Homer learned to harmonize his herd of goats with the Comfort Flame. In his next embodiment he began to use the Comfort Flame when only thirteen years of age, he was assigned to harmonize seven thousand people through the use of the Comfort Flame; he sustained that for some forty years. Soon after that He made the Ascension.

His particular virtue is Comfort which He gives to mankind and all life on Earth. His symbol is the white dove. The Dove represents the Maha Chohan Who is the representative of the Holy Spirit. His banner is purple; upon it is the emblem of the white dove from which eminate seven rays. Ivy which is a symbol of everlasting life, seems to be a favorite of His and much used by Him. He usually wears a white robe and white turban with a topaz on the forehead of the turban. The topaz is very frequently used by Him. He has golden hair and His eyes are amber color. He uses the fragrance of cinnamon. His keynote is "Homing".

MANU

The position of Manu is a first ray activity.

The seven principal mental qualities for mastery are represented by the Seven Manus.

A Manu is a wholly perfect Being Who (with the Twin Ray) takes on the responsibilities and acts as God-Parent of a root race and its sub-races. He becomes the pattern or prototype (archtype) for that whole race. Sub-races are the seven divisions of a root race, each one predominantly of individuals of one of the seven rays.

The first, second and third root races have completed their evolution on Earth, made the Ascension and gone on into greater activities in the scheme of things, as have also the Manus of these three races.

The Manus of the four remaining root races are still working with the Earth, as They cannot go on until each one's race has as a whole completed its evolution on Earth, or unless some other Beings take Their place.

The present Manus are,

Lord Himalaya of the fourth root race,
Lord Vaivasvata of the fifth root race,
Lord Meru of the sixth root race,
The Divine Director of the seventh root race.

There are still some of the fourth root race people who have not completed their course or evolution here on Earth. The fifth root race (Aryan race) is progressing on Earth at present. A small number of the sixth root race are in embodiment, and the seventh root race is to begin coming in. They have been waiting at inner levels for a very long time; of course progressing and expanding their consciousness and light there. Therefore they are already greatly developed lifestreams with much accumulated good in their Causal Bodies.

Ascended Masters and great Beings such as a Manu,

when it is said that They incarnate, it is another action
of the Law than that of a human being incarnating or
taking embodiment. They do not need it for Themselves. In such a case the Being takes over a physical
body (and works through it), which has been inhabited
and prepared by another individual, who as a rule is
a "close" student or chela of the great Being. The chela
would be working in such close cooperation in full consciousness with the Being (Lord Maitreya worked in
this manner with Jesus). While the chela is asleep the
Being does at times use the body. Then there is another
action which is very rare, when a Being takes on a physical
body prepared by the chela but the chela has departed
from that body.

VAIVASVATA

Vaivasvata is Manu of the fifth root race, the prototype
for this race. His action now is the redemption and
development of the lifestreams of this race which is His
responsibility. The people are those of the Aryan type.

He is tall and very stately. He is around six feet eight
inches in height, has brown hair and brown eyes. His
Focus on Earth is in the Himalayan Mountains.

THE DIVINE DIRECTOR

The Divine Director is a Great Cosmic Being, Who
is authority for the conditions of Earth.

When mankind began to turn from the light He was
rendering service in a similar capacity as a messenger.

He pointed out what their attention could lead them into; which has resulted in the difference between Them and us now—just thought and feeling, it can be summed up to attention, then feeling will follow. Mankind would not listen. He refused to go the way of mankind but instead attained His eternal freedom and is now today such a great authority in the worlds of the people of Earth.

He was Saint Germain's Teacher and He is the One known at inner levels as the Master "R". He is the One Who founded the House of Rakoczy. Saint Germain working under Him and with Him in a similar manner as Jesus worked with Lord Maitreya, Saint Germain carried out His service and used His name during a time, in middle Europe.

The Divine Director observes every lifestream at a certain point and when they can be of assistance to mankind He transmutes their human creation. That is the reason for the Cave of Light in India where many have been freed through the centuries. He is the authority to determine whose human creation may be consumed and transmuted for him or her and to what extent, in part or completely. He has for more than two hundred thousand years assisted lifestreams to perfect the outer manifestation of themselves.

He now gives His assistance to students in the outer world. He has transmuted the human creation of many hundreds of students since this instruction came forth. In classes He would draw the power of light from the Cave of Light there in India.

He will enfold one in His light rays and transmute the shadows. One can call to Him to set aside time and space, which means to be set free from the pressure of human creation in the atmosphere; and the transmuting of one's own human creation sets him free from that. The eternal *now* is the absence of time and space, a state of consciousness with only the Presence—God in action. Ascended Masters do not recognize time and space as we know it; distance is not considered by Them.

He started the action of projecting a disc of light into the emotional bodies of all young people in America in 1937. This acted for all the students too. It is a violet disc about the size of a dinner plate, which rotates, drawing the discord in the feeling world into it. The inner action of it is similar as to what liquid light would do.

He enfolded every sincere student, when He first came forth in an action of the Three-fold Flame which He placed around them; It is larger than the physical body. Give recognition to it and visualize the Three-fold Flame in the heart expand and become one with It.

He will give assistance in expanding the "Golden Man" in the heart (which is a replica of one's own Christ Self when his light has expanded beyond a certain point), and the point of light in every cell; expanding the power of light in each one.

The Divine Director represents the seventh root race. His is the responsibility and authority for this race. It is for this reason that He has during the past twenty years or so gone to such tremendous effort to give assistance to free as many individuals as possible, in an endeavor to set up actions that would bring about the redemption and complete purification of Earth, setting all mankind free, thereby providing a place for His root race to embody and complete their evolution.

He is a Member of the Karmic Board, representing the first ray.

He represents an action similar to the Christ Self (Higher Mental Body) to mankind.

He will give assistance to adjust things in legal matters.

He is around six feet, four inches in height.

LORDS (GODS) OF THE MOUNTAINS

The Lords or Gods of the Mountains are great Cosmic Beings. They are guardians of certain mountain ranges. They govern the atmosphere. They can be called into action to clear the air currents and the atmosphere and control weather conditions.

LORD HIMALAYA

Lord Himalaya is known in the East as Chakshusha. He is Manu of the fourth root race. He is in charge of the Retreat of the Blue Lotus; and guardian of the Permanent Ray of the masculine aspect. The presentation of Truth has been predominantly mental (masculine), in the past, because the Masculine Ray was the stimulus for spiritual unfoldment and the seekers of Truth have been magnetized and gone within its radiance. Now as the currents change at inner levels to the Feminine Ray there will be more and more tendency to emotional control and development of the feeling nature.

He is a Teacher of teachers. He is the Teacher of those who aspire to become Buddhas.

Lord Himalaya works with Aries in the purifying of the atmosphere of Earth.

Lord Himalaya and other Ascended Beings directed the decrees and songs which were given in class into the mental and feeling worlds of mankind. He also opened air currents through which was carried the class work to people in India especially; but the air currents were so arranged that the instruction could be heard throughout the world by those attuned to listen. He insulated the air currents through which He directed the message given in class in California on October 10, 1938 (for the first time); no destructive forces could tune in on that.

Lord Himalaya governs the energy in the Himalayan Mountains. There has been a power and blessing in the Himalayan Mountains through the ages which was nowhere else.

The Holy river in India in which people are healed, is a certain section of the Ganges River. This part the Masters keep purified, charged and controlled through Their radiation and action. It was said that the Masters took gold from the Himalayan Mountains, put it through a process by which it became vapor-like and released it into the Ganges there.

Lord Himalaya was Lord Gautama's, Lord Maitreya's

and Kuthumi's Teacher. He is about seven feet two inches in height. His radiance has been very tangible at times, it has appeared as golden snow.

LORD MERU

Lord Meru is the Manu of the sixth root race. He is in charge of the Retreat in Mount Meru in the Andes Mountains in South America, and is guardian of the Permanent Ray of the feminine aspect.

His action is illumination. He has a great power of influence in working with the Beings of the elements.

He is about seven feet in height. He and His Twin Ray the Goddess Meru both have blue eyes and golden hair.

LORD TABOR

Lord Tabor governs all mountain ranges in North and Central America.

Mount Tabor which was named after Him, was His Retreat in the Holy Land in Jesus' time. Shortly after Jesus made the Ascension He came and took charge of the Rocky Mountains in the United States of America where He has His Retreat now.

Lord Tabor is around eight feet in height. His fragrance is that of pine.

LORD OF THE SWISS ALPS

Lord of the Swiss Alps is guardian of those mountains. He is also of large stature.

LORD OF NATURE AND LORD OF GOLD

The Lord (God) of Nature and Lord of Gold came forth April 7, 1939, this being the first time in history that They have taken any direct action for mankind's progress. It was only through sufficient understanding and application of the students that made this possible. Their coming forth brought about a great release in power, intelligence and in the elemental kingdom—earth, water, air and fire—they govern the action of supply and release it where and when obedience to the light is given.

The Lord of Gold is the standard of the world, and gold is His scepter. He is the governor of that element.

The Lord of Nature is about six feet in height. He governs the powers of nature. He has much to do with vegetation and fruits. To redeem nature call to the Lord of Nature and Lord Tabor.

POLARIS AND MAGNUS

The Great Cosmic Beings Polaris and Magnus are Twin Rays (or Flames), Who represent the poles and axis to the Earth at this time. The axis is a current of energy—a light ray from Polaris' heart to Magnus; as the Two Permanent Rays form the matrix for the heart for the Earth, Polaris and Magnus form the axis. Polaris, the masculine aspect, color blue, is at the north pole and Magnus, the feminine aspect, is at the south pole, which gives forth a pink and gold radiance. They govern and control the axis of the Earth which forms a similar action to the Earth as does the spine to the body. Polaris and Magnus have assisted and have been instrumental in keeping the spines of mankind erect. They hold the action of the world in the palms of Their hands, so to speak.

Polaris with the Lord Maha Chohan releases energy in nature, and can command the Beings of the Elements to act on the instant.

There is an action from the Star Arcturus in conjunction with the Star Polaris which is a balancing action.

We can call for and use Polaris' Cloak of Invisibility around our bodies, possessions and property.

COSMIC BEING HARMONY

Harmony is a Cosmic Being and Harmony is His Cosmic Name. He is from the Seventh Sphere, and was the first One to come forth from that Sphere of action. He is the Cosmic representative of that quality to the Earth.

He represents the Law of Harmony—harmony of music, machinery and industry. He was a good mechanic in one embodiment. He is the authority for harmony in all nature, and when there is enough harmony established on Earth even the deserts will put forth flowers several times a year.

Harmony is the Great Tenor Who sang from the globe of light in one of the Retreats on one occasion when some of Saint Germain's chelas were present in their inner bodies.

He had not contacted the people of Earth for a long

time. His real work with the Earth only began after much of the cleansing process had taken place. He gave a dictation on January 2, 1938, and started a definite action of assistance to the students.

He has offered to assist students in maintaining harmony if they will call to Him.

COSMIC BEING VICTORY

Victory is the Cosmic Being from Venus Who issued the fiat which set aside the old occult laws for the Earth. He responded to Saint Germain's calls for assistance for the Earth.

He has not known anything but victory in any effort of His for thousands of centuries. He is the authority of victory for Earth.

He came forth into outer action in nineteen thirty-seven to give Earth assistance until she is victorious.

He invited the students to His Garden of Victory; to go there while their bodies sleep. Sanat Kumara was His great Teacher. His predominant action is love, His quality is Victory, and also forgiveness. He is about six feet six inches in height.

RAY-O-LIGHT

This Cosmic Being came forth for the first time September 10, 1939, and gave a discourse; He had not contacted the people of Earth for a very long time.

His action is to speak and present unadulterated truth; which comes with *enough* light—a ray of light.

His particular activity is to remove fear and doubt which must be transmuted before the full power and action of light can manifest for the individual or mankind and the planet. Fear is the acceptance that there is an opposing force, but fearlessness is all light with no opposite. Fearlessness is an action of the fire element and makes one feel very comfortable, as well as courageous.

He is the authority over the action of fear and selfishness. When all fear is removed there will be no more selfishness. He will help remove the feeling of fear. His quality is fearlessness, a complete absence of fear, which gives one a feeling of calm mastery.

He has legions of Angels and Beings of the elements at His command.

One can call for His light substance and Cosmic Flame of Fearlessness to enfold oneself.

LANTO

Lanto was the Emperor Chan of China during a time of great light and a magnificent age. It was said that was during the time of Confucius, a Chinese philosopher (551-479 B. C.), and that He made the Ascension at that time. He stressed honesty and integrity among the people which is still outstanding in China in spite of the degraded, limited and fanatical conditions there today. These conditions in China as well as in India came about through the priesthood. Some of this perhaps was shown in the pictures known as "Fu Manchu". The only hope to remedy these distortions is this release of the ever increasing Cosmic Light.

Chan is a Chinese word for perfection. Lanto was a chela of Lord Himalaya. He stressed the expansion of the light in his heart during his development and intensified it to a point to where it was visible through his flesh. He then insisted that it would never recede but would ever increase in intensity and forever be visible through his body. He accomplished that which no other Master of Earth has and in this respect He is unique among the Ascended Masters.

Lanto was One of the Ascended Masters Who stood with the Ascended Master Saint Germain from the beginning of the bringing forth of this instruction to mankind, that there were those in the outer world who could respond. The Ascended Masters do at all times cooperate One with Another, but They were not all aware and sufficiently familiar with the circumstances involved, being occupied in other fields.

He has been in charge of the Retreat in the Grand Teton for a long time and was the presiding Master at the Conclaves held there. He is now prepared to go on into greater service. The Being known as Confucius was prepared and ready to take His place, but Lord Lanto decided to remain until the change of the axis. However, He did relinquish this position and assumed Chohanship of the second ray in July nineteen fifty-eight, instead of going on into greater spheres of service.

His particular quality is reverence of life—creation. His keynote is "O! Thou Sublime Sweet Evening Star" from Tannhauser. He uses the fragrance of sandalwood.

Lord Confucius assumed the position of Hierarch of the Teton Retreat after the ceremonies held there on the Fourth of July. He is also on the second ray.

THE COSMIC BEING COSMOS

Cosmos is a great Cosmic Being and comes from the Source of all Intelligence to Earth. He came forth July 22, 1939, in a Cosmic Action in connection with the great release of Cosmic Light to the Earth. Two Secret Rays were sent with Him. These are in addition to the Seven, this makes nine and the action of the Power of the Three times Three.

Cosmos is the authority for one of these Rays. He enfolded every student in these Rays and then everyone on Earth.

The color of the Two Rays was not revealed but they are of colors not known on Earth. They will only be revealed when we have advanced sufficiently into the New Age, and that will end the need for armies, hospitals and institutions of incarceration.

One Ray operates from within out and the other from without in. They are enfolded in a blue radiance so the operation may not be observed by destructive forces— hence they are called secret.

Cosmos' coming forth changed the activity of the Laws

for the people of Earth. He and the Goddess of Justice
are in command of the activity of the Earth; They with
Saint Germain make a three-fold action.

The release of these Rays gave enough assistance in addition to the calls being made by the students, to hold the
balance against the destructive forces.

He said that it was commanded that K-17 add many
more to His Legions.

Cosmos is *one* with our lifestreams, He represents to
us the same as our own lifestream.

Cosmos also has much to do with music.

ZARATHUSTRA

The Zarathustras represent the spirit of fire, the Sacred
Fire. They are the Beings that carried or represented
that action to Earth. They are an authority over the fire
element. They taught the religion of fire, and have been
known for it down through the ages.

It has been said there have been twenty-nine Zarathustras; not necessarily embodiments of the same lifestream; but as the Christ activity has been embodied
by various individuals, Zoroaster perhaps being the last
of These (around 600 B. C. or more). Zarathustra is in
command of Beings of the fire element. His particular
quality is enthusiasm.

PRINCIPA

This great Being is the Lord of Divine Order, known
at inner levels as Principa. He represents divine order.

He has been in the great Silence since the laggards came and disorder was created.

He came forth December 15, 1957, to give assistance to those who will call to Him, in establishing divine order again; divine order in thought, in the emotional world, affairs, business, homes and surroundings. Mankind and the Earth need divine order very much and it must be brought about in order to have the full expression of the incoming age, the seventh ray which is ordered service.

GODDESS OF LIBERTY

The Statue of Liberty in reality represents a great Cosmic Being—a Goddess, Whose radiance is felt by everyone who comes into the New York harbor.

France gave the assistance to free America from England and she also gave the Statue of Liberty which stands in the New York harbor. It is in France where is the Retreat in which is established the Liberty Flame. Its radiance induced France to give that assistance.

It was the Goddess of Liberty Who appered to General Washington in a Vision in the winter of 1777, in that hour of our country's greatest need, and showed him the destiny of America. How did She know then it would be fulfilled and that the destruction of America could be averted? Such things can be known by Cosmic Beings through the Cosmic Light which is a great mirror on which is thrown the activity of life.

The Goddess of Liberty issued the decree in that

vision, for the Light as of a thousand suns to descend, to prevent the third episode. This has been done through the release of this Cosmic Light which brought about the required response from some of mankind, sufficient to accomplish this. Thus was it made possible to hold the balance for the Earth against the destructive forces. Otherwise it would have resulted in a great cataclysm.

The Goddess of Liberty is the One Who secured the dispensation for the release of the Cosmic Light. When She interceded for the Earth She explained the conditions and the requirements; then She was given authority in regards to the Earth which had not been given to any Being outside the Central Sun before. She came forth into action in the nineteen thirties, after the old occult laws had been set aside and the atmosphere began to be rapidly transformed. This was Her action in the Freedom for the Earth and all life upon it.

Liberty and Freedom are the two Qualities our America stands for.

Every individual, just after individualization, receives liberty of actions (Liberty is a Cosmic Virtue) through the Presence of the Goddess of Liberty, and again, just before taking the first embodiment; then, too, before each succeeding embodiment.

The Goddess of Liberty is One of the Twelve Beings around the Sun. Her Cosmic Quality is Liberty; Her obligation is to keep it and the love of Liberty alive and active in the evolutions on the planets of the system.

Her interest is to appease the heavy-laden and weary

ones as is a mother's tendency, and transmute as much human creation for them as possible. She is the Cosmic Mother for the people of America and the Earth.

She is much larger in stature than the people of Earth. She usually wears white with blue.

PALLAS ATHENA

Most of these names used in mythology are names of *real* and great Beings, Who were known and associated with mankind before the density grew so great that the contact was lost. Mythology is a semblance of man's memories with much perversion and human concepts woven around them.

Pallas Athena is the Goddess of Truth. She was seen by and counselled with the people on Lemuria before the veil of maya was created through thought and feeling. As the maya grew Their forms became more and more indistinct until They could no longer be seen by the people. The memory of Them remained only in myth and fable, except for the various avatars and messengers.

Truth, itself, has perhaps been misrepresented more than any other quality or activity among the people of Earth. Pallas Athena is the representative of Cosmic Truth to the Earth. She was vested by the Sun Goddess with the Virtue of Truth and accepted the responsibility to sustain it for the people.

Pallas Athena was the High Priestess in the Temple of Truth on Atlantis. People seeking Truth and desiring enlightenment on education, science, governmental activities or whatever their service was in their localities, would come to this Temple where they absorbed the radiance from the Flame of Truth.

She withdrew more and more from the knowledge of mankind as the shadows grew and was then completely forgotten by the masses.

All messengers who give Truth to mankind are under the radiation and guidance of Pallas Athena.

She is a Member of the Karmic Board and was honorary Spokesman for the year of nineteen fifty-seven, because She was One of the Sponsors for the year. She and the Lord Maha Chohan are Twin Rays. Truth and Comfort are the two facets of the one Flame. She has golden hair. Her Keynote is "Homing".

PORTIA

Portia is the Goddess of Justice and also Goddess of Opportunity. She represents divine justice to the Earth. Her action is that of balance, with the scales as a symbol; there must be harmony to hold a balance.

She went on into perfection, when imperfection began to be externalized, and She was therefore not drawn into discord with mankind. She remained in the inner spheres and only came forth April 9, 1939, for the first time. She started Cosmic Justice into action for the Earth, which must reign supreme once again. It was made known then that She was the Twin Ray of beloved Saint Germain.

She is One of the Members of the Karmic Board, representing the Seventh Ray on that Board. She became

Spokesman June 27, 1954, in honor of Saint Germain having become the presiding Master for the next two thousand year cycle.

One can call to Her for assistance in legal action.

Her electronic pattern is the Maltese Cross.

GODDESS OF PEACE

The Goddess of Peace represents Peace to the Earth. She came into the atmosphere of Earth May 19, 1938, for the first time, to render service in cooperation with the Goddess of Liberty. She came from the inner spheres where She had abided for thousands of centuries (since after the second Golden Age), not coming to Earth because there was not enough light and understanding in mankind. She came because of the calls—the decrees given by the students, through which enough of the cleansing process had taken place.

She will enfold one in Her golden flaming substance when given recognition and the call is made.

GODDESS OF PURITY

The Goddess of Purity represents the quality of Purity to the Earth.

She went forward at the time mankind receded from the light and entered the great Silence where She has abided since after the second golden age. She was driven, so to speak, from the Earth because She expressed the quality of Purity which the people did not desire sufficiently any more, and even today do not welcome too much.

The Goddess of Purity came forth into action January 1, 1939, for the first time since She entered into the great Silence when mankind became too impure. The Angelic Host came into the atmosphere of Earth when She came; They preceded Her for hours. Around eighty thousand years ago She came and looked the Earth over but returned as there was too little desire for purity at the time.

She works from and abides in the Etheric City over Arizona (U. S. A.). She also has a Focus on the Island of Madagascar. Her flower is the lily.

AMARYLLIS

Amaryllis is the Goddess of Spring. She has legions of elementals and Angels at Her command. Each year under Her direction comes forth the beautiful Spring. She came to Earth with Her legions and produced the Spring each year for nine hundred years before mankind began to inhabit the planet, and has produced each Spring since.

KWAN YIN

Kwan Yin Who is well known in China is an Ascended Being although that is not generally known among the Chinese. She is still remembered by the people of China, in spite of the density they have been drawn into, from that time long ago when She walked among Her people in Her perfected tangible body. She is responsible for the honesty and integrity among the Chinese.

Kwan Yin is known as the Goddess of Mercy. Her particular God-Quality is Mercy. She directs the Flame of Mercy and Compassion. Mercy means there is more assistance given through love than merit earned. Her services to mankind are mercy and healing; these two really go together. She is One of Those Who are in charge of directing the healing activity to the mankind of Earth. She is grateful to be called to, for Her forgiveness, mercy, compassion and healing. She also renders great service to the incoming children. Kwan Yin is patroness of women and of birth. One can call to Her for assistance to overcome the tendencies to create discord.

She received the crown of Chohan of the Seventh Ray for the two thousand year cycle, fourteen thousand years ago. She remained as Chohan of the Seventh Ray until Saint Germain took over the Chohanship.

She is in charge of the Temple of Mercy in China. She is a Member of the Karmic Board, representing the Sixth Ray on that Board; and served as Spokesman for a short time, several years ago.

Lord Gautama was Her Master. It was said that She maintained life in the body for one thousand years before ascending. Since Her attainment was through the feminine aspect She was drawn within the Feminine Ray focused through Mount Meru and given inner training there.

Her flower and electronic pattern are five-petaled lotus.

ROSE OF LIGHT

The Ascended Master Rose of Light was mentioned September 23, 1938, for the first time. She gave a discourse March 27, 1939, to the students.

She represents the quality which gives Her the Name Rose of Light. That quality causes the light in the heart to expand—as a flower unfolds its petals.

She represents the activity of the heart. Her action is to discern truth. It is the heart action which is the activity of the I AM Presence in the body and it (the heart) is the real knower of truth.

When some thought, idea or conception comes to one's consciousness from the heart there is a feeling of perfect rest and peace when testing it out in contemplation, but when there is rebellion or disturbed feelings, that is an indication there is something wrong.

VIRGO

Virgo, the Goddess of Earth, is a Cosmic Being Who provided the substance of earth, which was all pure in the beginning, something like alabaster or white quartz radiating iridescent colors of the rainbow. The activity of the structure of the Earth is under Her direction, as are the Gnomes, the Beings of the earth element.

Virgo represents the earth element, that is, the substance of the planet and the elements of the physical body. It is Her substance which holds the water element. The purification and raising of the earth or mineral element into light substance comes under Her direction and it is Her responsibility.

Virgo, to some extent, is the Cosmic Mother of all who embody on the planet Earth, since their physical bodies are composed of Her element.

She nourishes nature along with the Lord Maha Chohan.

Virgo and Pelleur are Twin Rays.

PELLEUR

The Cosmic Being Pelleur is the Directing Intelligence of the activities in the center of the Earth. It is a place of great perfection and a great Focus of Light. There is no night there but a soft white radiance of even pressure and perfect climatic conditions all the time. It is a harmonious and very peaceful place.

The people that live there do not have any discord. When lifestreams take embodiment there that do have some discordant karma, they are consulted about it and with their permission it is transmuted. They are taught how to live harmoniously and not generate discord.

From Pelleur's region much assistance is being given on the surface of the Earth. Light rays are being directed from there to the surface and in cooperation with the Cosmic Light they are assisting in the cleansing activity of the Earth and the bringing forth of perfection. His activity is a balancing action.

NEPTUNE AND LUNARA

Neptune is a Cosmic Being Who supplies the substance of the water element for the Earth. Water is a condensation of substance from the Central Sun. He is the Director of that element and therefore the substance of our emotional bodies also comes under His direction as do, too, the Undines, the Beings of the water element.

Neptune's Twin Ray is Lunara and They together govern the tides. Her action in relation to the moon is similar as is Virgo's to the Earth.

Neptune gives to every human being the capacity to hold a balance within the emotional body (feelings), the control of which is governed by the Three-fold Flame in the heart.

ARIES AND THOR

Aries is a Cosmic Being Who created the atmosphere, and governs and directs the element of air for the Earth— air which is our very breath.

Illumination and inspiration are activities and services rendered by Her through the air element.

The four elements are used in creating any planetary system. A manifestation is enfolded in the element of air which also interpenetrates it.

Aries has charge of the activity of purifying the atmosphere of Earth. The purification of the atmosphere includes the minds of the people. It is the discord generated by mankind and radiated into the atmosphere that obscures our hearing and seeing at a distance, which would be unlimited otherwise.

Sound is governed by Aries. Music, sound, fragrance, et cetera, is carried from one place to another through the air element. It is conveyed by the Sylphs, the Beings of the air, which is their service. The blessings from the Ascended Ones too come to us on the air element and the blessings we send out to others are also conveyed through the air under the direction of Aries.

The substance of air is radiation of/from the Threefold Flame in the Sun drawn to produce the atmosphere. This establishes a balance from without with the Flame action in the heart, which manifests as breath which naturally is rhythmic.

Aries came forth September 22, 1938, for the first time; that was at Saint Germain's request.

The Cosmic Being, Thor, Who is the Twin Ray of Aries, governs the creation of the Four Winds and directs their actions.

OROMASIS AND DIANA

Oromasis and Diana are Beings of the fire element Who served One of the Ascended Masters for a long time and then they were endowed with immortality, took physical embodiment and are now ascended. They are sometimes referred to as Prince Oromasis and Diana, Goddess of Fire.

The Beings of the four elements are created as such,

and are not an Individual Three-fold Flame from the Sun,
as is mankind. When an Ascended Being offers them
the Three-fold Flame and they accept it, that makes them
immortal, as man is.

Oromasis and Diana work with beloved Saint Germain.
They also work from Hercules' Retreat. They minister
to and quicken the activity of the Three-fold Flame in
individuals. They will also intensify the Violet Flame at
one's call, or any action of the Flame.

Oromasis went through physical embodiment to get
what was required to make the Ascension, but he did
not allow himself to be drawn into discord.

He has Legions of Angels of Blue Lightning at His
command. He works mostly with His own element. His
scepter is a Rod of White Lightning.

Oromasis along with Astrea and Archangel Michael,has
been rendering tremendous service in cleansing and transmuting psychic substance and discordant conditions. He
will give assistance in clearing the brain of the dense
substance created through the use of wrong foods and
drink and especially tobacco. He can be called into a
room to walk through it, purify and clear the atmosphere,
just by the radiance of His Flame. He is always ready
to render that service when the call is made.

Oromasis was able to harmonize the Beings of the four
elements enough by nineteen thirty-nine so that they
would cooperate and not return the destruction upon
mankind, which would have resulted in cataclysmic action.
When they are harmonized sufficiently they will no longer

cause any storms or other destructive actions of nature.

This Diana, and the One with the Eloah Arcturus, are two different lifestreams.

MARY, MOTHER OF JESUS

Mary started her life of consecration early. She started Temple life at about three years of age, having been put there by Her over-zealous parents, apparently several years too young for such training. Her own strength of light with the assistance of the Archangels which was permitted by the great law under a special dispensation by Lord Maitreya, enabled her to come out successfully.

The Archangels, with Angels, would often visit her during her childhood when she was alone, and instruct her. They were her conscious companions and friends.

Mary was given special training in concentration. She had much training in the Nature Temples at inner levels previous to that lifetime. She learned how to work with elemental life. She works close with nature and elemental life now, and has a certain action with plant life. She was responsible for bringing into existence here on Earth the maiden-hair fern. She drew forth the picture of it, concentrated on it and elemental life outpictured it in the physical and has sustained its growth.

Her embodiment as Mother of Jesus was in the divine plan long before she entered the physical realm. She went through a severe initiation at inner levels to test her strength some time before taking embodiment; this affording her that opportunity.

Mary met Joseph soon after she had been released from the Temple. Archangel Gabriel assisted her as to the service she was to render and gave her the vision of Jesus Christ before His birth. She was so attentive in consciousness to the Divine Beings and maintained harmony in her feelings, which enabled her to get the directions given, is why Archangel Gabriel said to her, "Hail, Mary full of grace". Gabriel conveyed to her that Jesus would be the Messiah and it was required of her to tell no one, not even the priest. Of course Joseph knew it.

When Jesus was a baby an Angel warned Joseph of the danger, and they fled to Egypt. Mary and Joseph followed the promptings—the inner directions they were given—such as going to Bethlehem for the birth of Jesus and fleeing to Egypt shortly thereafter. If they had not given such obedience the Christian Movement would never have been; and they would have just lived out their natural lives as holy men and women. Their mission would have had to be carried out by some one else later.

Mary, understanding the Law, vowed then, to assist every one of those lifestreams who had lost their lives (by order of King Herod) to their Ascension. They abided, for a time, near Karnak, and when Jesus was able to understand the simpler workings of the Law, they were directed to apply for entrance to the Temple there, to which Mary took Him each day. Some years later they returned to Jerusalem.

Mary and Jesus were aware of and communed with the Angels and Ascended Beings.

Mary gave tremendous protection to Jesus all through His life. She always held the concept of the Perfection He was to outpicture, and through His trials and crucifixion She was His stabilizing power. He asked Her before His Ascension to stay and hold the focus He had established until the teaching could be spread, and anchored sufficiently that it could be sustained during the two thousand year period.

At the time of Jesus' Ascension She became the Cosmic Mother for all unascended mankind.

Mary, the disciples, and some friends, fixed up a building at Bethany after Jesus' Resurrection, and formed a colony; later others joined them. That was their home for the next thirty years or more.

Mary and John, and sometimes others, had a daily communion on the Hill of Bethany, through which Jesus assisted them and directed their activities.

Sometime after Jesus' Ascension, Mary, some of the disciples, and some others journeyed to Egypt where Mary visited Luxor again. Then they went on to the Island of Crete, where they drew the currents for the future work of Paul the Apostle. They, but particularly Mary, visited and drew the currents at various places such as Fatima and Lourdes which were to be brought into action later; from France they went to the British Isles. Jesus appeared to them there and thus there was established a focus into which King Arthur tuned some centuries later. The "Grail" was left at Glastonbury.

They drew a focus of light in Ireland which assisted Saint Patrick in that future time to establish Christianity there. They returned to Bethany by way of the Mediterranean Sea.

Mary, in that embodiment many times saw the word "Persevere" in the atmosphere, and also on the waters on their way to England.

Her life was one of initiations; and to sum up Her life, in one word, for that lifetime, would be "solitude".

It is said that She is the Twin Ray of Archangel Raphael and so She is of the Angelic kingdom. One can readily see why She had so many experiences and close association with the Angels and Archangels. Being an Archaii also explains Her great power, and, since She is of the Fifth Ray, gives reason for Her great concentration.

Mary was also drawn, on the inner, before Her Ascension, to the Brotherhood of Mount Meru, and within the Permanent Ray of the feminine aspect, there to receive training.

When Her time came to depart from this realm She had a little ceremony with the people of the colony. They carried out Her request and Her body was placed in the tomb after passing; when they opened the tomb, three days later, all they found was white roses, one for each person of the colony. At inner levels (after Her Ascension) She was crowned Queen of Heaven, for the Christian Dispensation, which, from a cosmic standpoint, made Her Mother of the world. This position She held until May nineteen fifty-four, when Saint Germain and Portia assumed the responsibilities for the incoming age. This came about through a certain experience in one embodiment which resulted in Her taking a definite stand to assist deformed children and their parents who have to take care of them.

She directs and assists at inner levels with the creation of the bodies, and especially, the heart of all incoming children. They are drawn to Her Temple of the Sacred Heart for preparation before taking embodiment. Motherhood is Her great service and purpose in life. Most of Her embodiments were in a feminine body.

Healing is another great service She renders mankind. She is One of the authorities of the healing activity to the Earth.

Mary portrayed standing with a snake under Her feet symbolizes complete control over the feelings and the five senses.

She directs Angels and has legions of Them at Her command. She is the representative of grace to mankind. She has golden hair and violet eyes. She usually wears soft blue garments and a veil over Her hair. Her Ascension is commemorated August fifteenth. Her Keynote is "Whispering Hope".

META

Meta is a guardian from Venus. She came to stay and assist Sanat Kumara until the Earth was assured of her freedom. She found, after several hundred years of serving and training at inner levels, that She had the greatest adaptability of the fifth sphere.

She and Her three children lived in Persia in their final embodiment on Earth. They all attained mastery and maintained their bodies for a long period of time. They were not so fortunate as is the student today, for they came under the old law and had to look upon some of their human creation. The paramount idea at that time was to perfect and maintain life in the body and only ascend after hundreds of years. Whereas now the action is to have the Ascension at the close of this embodiment, the natural span of life. Meta was the first to make the Ascension, then She was able to give the others assistance which enabled them to ascend soon thereafter.

Her Son Cha Ara is the only One of the children Who is known of in the outer world.

Meta has worked from the fifth sphere through the centuries; Her main service being healing, but giving instructions on Truth as well, which gives the healing of the mind. In that sphere She taught the use of the light rays which is a science. At first She worked with and taught disembodied individuals in those inner realms. Later She decided to establish Temples of Healing in the Etheric Cities, from which selfless Beings could, by the projection of light rays, transmute some of the disease, epidemics and such like in general, in the vicinity over which the Etheric Cities abide.

She worked as associate Chohan with the presiding Chohan of the Fifth Ray for about five hundred years and then assumed the full Chohanship as that Great Being went on to greater service. She served in this capacity for several thousand years.

Her special activity is to assist to perfect our bodies.

She returns with Sanat Kumara to Venus.

CHA ARA

Cha Ara in His last embodiment was a son of Meta, they lived in Persia. He attained mastery in his physical body. He was able to produce the elixer of life; first through substance of the physical world, then through precipitation direct from the universal, and he would give it to people. He maintained that body for several hundred years before He made the Ascension.

He gave a dictation as early as December 25, 1932, over the light and sound ray. He has a certain responsibility to America; the destructive forces shall be removed and He shall see Her victorious.

He was also One Who stood with Saint Germain in the beginning of His giving this instruction to mankind.

He was One Who walked the streets of some of our cities in December nineteen thirty-seven to help give the needed protection at the time.

His particular quality is joy. He gives one the feeling that everything is going to be right; and gives His feeling of authority over the human. One can call to Him when confronted with problems.

He uses the fragrance of roses.

LETO

Leto made the Ascension over three hundred years ago. She has golden hair. Calm determination is a natural characteristic of Hers. The fragrance of heather will be noticed about Her many times. It became dear to Her through a particular experience when She was living in Scotland in the eleventh century.

When Godfre' and the others with him were enroute to France She appeared on the steamboat and traveled with them, teaching them on the way.

She will assist students to retain the memory of their activities while out of the body during sleep, if they will call to Her. Her unique service is Her adaptability to lovingly teach students on the Path to consciously leave the body and return at will. The Cloak of Invisibility is an action for which we may call to Her.

Healing is one of Her services also. In Europe, during a plague, She endeavored to give assistance but was not getting the needed results. The Cosmic Being, the Divine Director, informed Her that She was not releasing the full activity of which She was capable, whereupon under His direction, She connected with and released the Cosmic Healing Flame, which caused the plague to be stopped, and within a few days the people were free from it.

She has rendered direct service to mankind for more than two hundred years.

She did speak of knowing many of the students, particularly those of English ancestry.

ALEXANDER GAYLORD

Mr. Gaylord and Leto are Twin Rays.

Mr. Gaylord was a Messenger for the Great White Brotherhood for a long time before his Ascension. He was a member of the Secret Service and very active in South America in the nineteen thirties. He was instrumental in preventing certain foreign elements to get action there.

Mr. Gaylord and Leto were both in embodiment in South America during the Inca civilization.

We were told in December, 1937, that He, too, made the Ascension.

GODDESS OF LIGHT

The Goddess of Light is a great Being Who offered to be our Cosmic Sister of Light. Although She attained Her Ascension but recently, She has at Her command a tremendous power of light which She gained through that terrific experience. It was said in nineteen thirty-nine that Her Ascension took place within a lifetime (about fifty or sixty years previous).

She performed such a tremendous part in removing discarnates from the Earth, especially in New York City, in the Autumn of nineteen thirty-nine, as well as giving great assistance in handling many destructive forces by Her great release of Light. She wields enormous power. In some ways She is permitted to wield power the other Ascended Masters may not.

Reference to Her experience is given here in order
to bear out certain points of the Law. A band of black
magicians * imposed upon her a certain condition of
deformity. The lower part of her body was transformed
yet she moved about with great speed. In Europe and
in the East many such things took place, but her case
was the only one in the Western Hemisphere. These black
magicians had been watching her for nearly seventy years,
watching to catch her off guard so they could strike and
drive in. She had maintained life in that body for more
than five hundred years. Her attainment was so great
that to ward off those destructive beings was an easy
matter. Here is a subtle point. The black magicians had
not accepted her attainment. This she did not realize
and unknowingly let down the guard by feeling too sure
of herself. She gave that experience to show that one
must be on guard constantly until the Ascension is attained. One's Christ Self will be (stand) the guard
when It is called into action daily. She lived in the Andes
in South America with her mother. She kept the condition concealed from everyone. Even her mother never
saw it. Her place of occupation was fixed with sort of a
counter behind which she stood and no one saw her form
below the waist. She said that from the time it hap-

---

* A black magician is one who had great training in occult laws but
failed, and then used that power for destructive purposes. The Law was
such that what understanding and attainment an individual had gained
could not be taken away from him. However, since this instruction has
come forth and many phases of the interpretation of the Law have been
changed, the action of becoming a black magician is no longer possible.

pened, from that moment henceforth she never looked downward, but always up.

She did very great healing work, and her place became known as the "Shrine of Glory". She lived in this condition for three hundred years before she was released. She could not pass through so-called death because she had learned to maintain life in that body. There is a certain phase of the Law that when one attains to that point he can no longer pass on (die) as human beings do, but must go through into the Ascension.

It was only when through an inner awareness an individual from San Francisco, California, went to South America and contacted her, that her release came. This, too, is a subtle point of the Law. That individual had a certain attunement with her which had been created through their association in former embodiments. This set up a certain inner action like two ends of a pole, as it were, which produced (or released) the currents of energy that released her from that condition; and her body was normal again. Soon after that she completed her Ascension. That man was the only person on Earth through whom that service could be rendered. Just like Godfré was the only one who could give that assistance to David Lloyd.

Her calls to remove the black magicians from Earth were fulfilled in nineteen thirty-nine. This was done through the calls made by the student body during a period of a few years.

After Her Ascension She became known as the "Goddess of Light". A Cosmic Being gave Her that name.

She has a particular momentum of light, gained through concentration. Because of that experience She was compelled to draw a great amount of light. In her Shrine of Glory she drew "light substance", and this did the healing.

We can call for Her power of light; this will be qualified by Her. She will give assistance in governmental conditions, having served in governments many times.

The Goddess of Light sang the song "Call to Light" every day after that infliction until her freedom came.

The activity of the Goddess of Light represents your freedom.

One can call to Her for the action of the Cloak of Invisibility.

There is a Being known as the God of Light; there was only mention made of Him a couple of times.

QUEEN OF LIGHT

The Queen of Light and the Goddess of Light are two separate Beings; both having a great concentrate of light.

There was little said about the Queen of Light. She has a momentum on a certain thing (quality or activity), which produces beautiful manifestations. She wields great powers of light, and utilizes Her action by radiating Her crystal light substance to clear the mental bodies of the students and all mankind. Her action can enfold a person like a star with rays going out like crystal lightning.

She will assist one to retain the memory of things experienced at inner levels while asleep; even though it is not remembered on awakening it may be recalled an hour or sometime later; it may be just a sudden awareness.

CUZCO

The great Being Cuzco is in charge of the Retreat northeast of Suva. His action is particularly concerned with holding a balance in regards to the changing of the axis of Earth which results in cataclysmic activity ordinarily. There are always great Intelligent Beings governing such activities and He is One of Them.

He took part in the removing of the disembodied individuals from the atmosphere of Earth, a part of His service to mankind.

He gave a discourse July 25, 1939; stressed the need of making application in order to be free, and conserving and not wasting one's energy.

CASIMIR POSEIDON

Casimir Poseidon is a great Ascended Being. He was emperor of a great civilization which existed between twelve and fourteen thousand years ago in South America along the Amazon. He was ascended then, and through His guidance that civilization reached a state of great perfection.

His activity or service to mankind is the expanding of the Flame in the heart and the expansion of their light.

He has heavy golden hair. His people also had golden

hair, violet blue eyes, were tall and erect and very intelligent. His keynote is "Indian Love Call".

CHANANDA AND NAJAH

Chananda is the Ascended Master in charge of the Retreat in India where the Cave of Light is located. He is Chief of the Indian Council of the Great White Brotherhood.

A little more than eighty thousand years ago Chananda and many of the students now in embodiment, lived where now is San Francisco. It was then known as the City of the Seven Hills. It was during the cataclysm then that the Golden Gate and harbor were brought into existence.

He is One of the five Who walked the streets of some of our cities in December nineteen thirty-seven to give assistance and protection required at that time.

His Sister Najah is also ascended and appears as a young girl to people in India, giving them instruction and assistance. However, they do not know that She is an Ascended Being. She is also carrying the light in China.

Her service is especially with young people. She came and gave a dictation on November 26, 1938, for the first time. She will give assistance in charging our feelings with eternal youth at our call.

DAPHNE AND ARION

Daphne is an Ascended Being of great determination and represents that quality to mankind.

She gave a Dictation on June 5, 1939, but we never

heard much about Her. She pointed out that through determination mankind could do much more than they usually do. She said for us to call to the Presence and insist on having the qualities or actions manifest for which we call; to insist on having results.

Daphne and Arion are Twin Rays and great musicians. They are radiant and Ascended Beings from the seventh sphere.

Daphne is the name of the Great Being Who was the magnetization of that action called the "compound".

ERIEL

Eriel is an Ascended Being Who has His Focus in the high mountains in Arizona. He has been there and held that Focus of Light for a very long time. He worked silently and was not known in the outer world until in the nineteen-thirties. It was only then that He began to act in outer affairs of our nation.

In August nineteen thirty-nine, when so many children were thrown out of embodiment in China, the Master Eriel and Fun Wey rendered tremendous service and more than ten thousand children attained the Ascension. Eriel took sixty to His Retreat for training so they too could make the Ascension at the close of that embodiment. He has also taken others there and assisted them to their Ascension.

He teaches in His Retreat the use of the light and sound ray, the expansion of their own light and many other actions of the Law.

He assisted in rendering China great service by establishing certain conditions which they hope will bring about purity and her perfection again.

He is around six feet one inch in height and has piercing dark eyes.

LORD (GOD) LING

Lord Ling as He is known, is an Ascended Being (Master) Whose particular God-quality is Happiness. The color of His Flame is bright gold.

At the time of the incoming cycle of the Fifth Ray he was Moses, the one who led the people across the Red Sea, and the one who brought forth the Commandments to his race, which were to be the "law" for that cycle of two thousand years. Moses was raised in the Egyptian court but left that way of life because he felt he had a mission to perform. While he was in the desert, Micah, the Angel of Unity, came to him, in Whose Presence he was made aware of his own I AM Presence and also that the real name of God was "I AM". It was then that he received the statement "I AM that I AM". Micah instructed him and directed his mission. Moses had contact with an Ascended Being Who rendered the service of parting the sea, through Him.

He did not attain the Ascension in that embodiment. But he did attain it in a later embodiment as Ananda. In his close association with Lord Gautama Buddha he learned that service must be rendered in love, which he did not learn as Moses. This makes for happiness. After

His Ascension He became the Chohan of the Fifth Ray. He held that position until Hilarion assumed that responsibility.

He is happy to assist anyone who will call to Him for joy and happiness.

The electronic pattern of that lifestream is a lotus; the keynote "The Palms".

MICAH—COSMIC ANGEL OF UNITY

Micah is the Angel of Unity Who is mentioned in Washington's Vision, on Whose forehead appeared the word "Union". He is One of Archangel Michael's Legion.

Micah is the Being that appeared to Moses in the burning bush. He is the Guardian Angel for the Jewish Dispensation (which began at that time), and He still guards that phase of teaching.

His action is that of "union" or unity.

JOHN, THE BELOVED

John the disciple of Jesus who was closest to Him, later became known as "John, The Beloved". He had the knowledge of the I AM Presence and understood the Law better than any of the other disciples.

In early life he and his brother James were placed under the guardianship of Joseph, and were greatly blessed in that association. Joseph belonged to the Essene Brotherhood, and he saw to it that John got training in that Order; the outer branch of which he entered at the age of fifteen. This prepared him for the service he was to render with Jesus and His mission on Earth. John saw Jesus once, while in the outer temple, as Jesus walked by into the inner temple. John, with his attention on Jesus, stopped his ceremony for a moment, thought and felt deeply within himself, that that man would be outstanding among all others, although he did not know of his future mission and association. John, at the time of his maturity, returned to outer world life. Remembering the mysteries he had learned, he seemed to be waiting for some certain, unknown call; as were also many others in the various localities. When the call went forth (of course this was on the inner), some heard it and responded; it was subtle and many are still waiting for that call and for the Messiah to come.

Now these two thousand years later we have again been at such a point; and when that call went forth in the early nineteen-thirties, yes, may responded but many more did not.

John and those who associated with Jesus learned much through radiation as well as from verbal expressions. Many things they pondered over long after Jesus had left them. John was the only disciple Jesus could talk with freely because He comprehended and knew what Jesus' mission was, the others did not.

He learned to draw forth and radiate Divine Love. That impersonal love was greatly needed among the followers of Jesus, especially during those years after Jesus had ascended. Mother Mary had been left in his care and through his love he was able to greatly assist Her, until

She too made the Ascension some thirty years after Jesus. Soon after that John also made the Ascension.

John and Mother Mary witnessed Jesus' Ascension along with many others. They had been made aware of the great event beforehand, Jesus having informed them. When Jesus had ascended John wondered what He would do without Him, but Mary was a great comfort, strength and courage to him, until he was anchored sufficiently within his own light to meet the Master. John had been trained on the inner while with the Essene Brotherhood and had become able to receive the words from the Archangels (as Mary did also); after Jesus' Ascension John could see Him and receive instruction from Him. He was in daily contact with Jesus, during the following thirty years, and grew more and more to look like Him. He wrote down the things Jesus gave him. He wrote Revelations and there is much more to them than what there is in the Bible. He said these writings were preserved on Earth yet today and would some day be brought forth.

John gave a discourse December 21, 1937, through Godfré Ray King which was the first time for Him to speak to the people of Earth since He made the Ascension.

He is the embodiment of Divine Love, that is His particular God-quality and service to mankind. We all need more Divine Love and now have the privilege of calling to Him.

Strauss' "Tales From Vienna Woods" is His keynote. His electronic pattern is a maltese cross.

DJWAL KUL

Djwal Kul was a Tibetan and was known by the name Gai Ben-Jamin in his youth in the early part of the Theosophical Society, that was before he became an adept. He is often referred to as the Master D. K. and is also known as "The Tibetan".

He was on Lemuria and before the continent sank accompanied Lord Himalaya as He took the treasures to the heart of Asia for safe-keeping. He embodied many times in the mountains of Asia and lived in the great Lamaseries there. He was Kleinias, the favorite pupil of Pythagoras, and the first chela of Lord Gautama Buddha. It is claimed that He was Aryasanga who translated the Sutras of Patanjali by Shankaracharya into English; He later gave an English paraphrase of them to Mrs. Alice Bailey.

Djwal Kul worked with Morya and Kuthumi in bringing forth Theosophy. He was devoted to Kuthumi and built himself a small house further up the ravine from Kuthumi's home at Shigatse, Tibet. He willingly served in any capacity, in whatever there was to be done, and through such service acquired the name "The Messenger of the Masters". It seems he has always preferred to stay in the background and avoid outer recognition as much as possible. He supplied much data for the book "The Secret Doctrine", and a large part of it was dictated by him. He precipitated several pictures during those days of Theosophy.

Djwal Kul, like Morya and Kuthumi, the other two

Wise Men, presumably could have attained the Ascension at the close of that embodiment; but did not complete it then in order to have the closer physical connection for that future service in connection with Theosophy. He attained mastery as Morya and Kuthumi had, to the point of suddenly appearing in a room without the door opening, seemingly out of the atmosphere.

He became an adept on the second ray. He completed the Ascension in the latter part of the nineteenth century.

Djwal Kul secured a dispensation to give that work to mankind; that which was given to Alice A. Bailey. He had to persuade her to take it; he had to write quite a bit Himself to convince her of the quality of the work and that it was authentic before she accepted it as Truth and consented to take the work. Thus the door to the Ascended Ones was again opened after having been closed when Theosophy ceased to function in that capacity; and much more law and spiritual understanding was given, which was a sequence to Theosophy.

The work had already been laid out at inner levels when Mrs. Bailey started to take it in nineteen nineteen; soon after the thirty years of work was done in nineteen forty-nine she departed from this world of form, having completed her service. The work brought in a new and wider field and also group work, particularly on the inner. Esoteric teaching has heretofore been obtainable to the student only by his acceptance of the teacher's authority and obedience to that one under oath and pledges. The relation between the disciple and the Master remains but with the coming forth of this presentation of spiritual understanding the former action began to change and discipleship training was begun in group action. That was the beginning of new age training.

Djwal Kul is more familiar with the working of the Hierarchy and the rays than are the other Masters. He is in charge of organized thought and wisdom and an authority on cycles.

His service is to teach, give the spiritual understanding and expand the knowledge of the Law. He gives great assistance to those seeking truth and to the healers who have the welfare of mankind at heart. He works with the Red Cross and such philanthropic movements. He instructs students of the various Masters thereby relieving Them of some of Their teaching work. He also works with the healing Devas and certain other Devic groups.

He is Sponsor for Lord Maha Chohan's Retreat at Ceylon. He is also Sponsor for Central Asia.

His keynote is "Aloha Oe". His electronic pattern is that of a hand with a torch similar to that of the Goddess of Liberty's.

K-17 AND HIS SISTER

K-17 is known by some as "Friend"; that is His Cosmic Name and His service to mankind. He is a "friend" in the real meaning of the word; that is His special service and along with it goes protection.

He was master (an unascended Master) before his Ascension, when he met Godfré as he got off the boat in

France in the autumn of 1931. He was not yet ascended but was soon to attain that state in the "Cave of Symbols" with the assistance of the Atomic Accelerator.

He answered Godfré's call and met him at the port, and gave the assistance required, then took Godfré with some others, to his Villa where he and his sister abided. His sister too was unascended and had attained mastery. He was three hundred and ten years of age, his sister was three hundred, and looked like a young girl.

We were told in nineteen thirty-nine that He was ascended now and that He was at the head of the Secret Service, both inner and outer. That He was one of few Who served in the outer world in the tangible body the greatest part of the twenty-four hours. Many may come forth for a short time, but He was moving among mankind constantly, releasing His radiation everywhere. It was also said that He had been head of the inner Secret Service for a long time, even before His Ascension. There is no higher power given to anyone in the outer than to the Secret Service; not even the President may interfere with that.

K-17 operates under a wholly different phase of the Law than Saint Germain; for protection He has more authority in the physical realm.

He is One to call to for protection; for protection of things as well as personal. One action of His protection is the "ring-pass-not". He has Legions at His command. He will assist greatly to have sinister activities revealed in our government and otherwise. He knows how to handle and put an end to such activities. He will also assist in legal actions.

He was the One that saved the Panama Canal from destruction when those submarines were sent there to destroy it in nineteen thirty-nine.

LEONORA

Leonora invented a radio before Her Ascension by which the interior of the Earth can be reached; in another operation it can tune in on any place on Earth as well as in Earth's etheric realm; and in its third phase it can reach the various planets of this system. They can converse with each other through that machine. She worked on it for seven embodiments, carrying the memory over from one life to the next. Three of these embodiments were feminine and four masculine.

The radio is in the Cave of Symbols, Saint Germain's Retreat.

Leonora was in embodiment in France, knew Lafayette at that time and came to the Cave of Symbols from there.

She is now an Ascended Being.

DAVID LLOYD

David Lloyd was one of the Lloyd's of London England. He was living in India when a Master (an unascended Master) came to him to give him some instruction as well as radiation for what was to follow. After the passing of his father he and his mother went back to England. He was then about twenty years of age. Later he came to America in search of the crystal cup the Master had told him about. The crystal cup from which he would drink and this would be the assistance he required to make the Ascension.

For about fifty years he was in search of his quest—the man with the crystal cup. During all these years there was an inner preparation going on. This preparation made his victory possible when one day on Mount Shasta he met the man (Godfre'Ray King), the one and only one through whom that service could be given. His gratitude was so very great for His Ascension and complete Freedom. Gratitude is the particular God-quality He manifests. He is the One to call to when we want more gratitude in our beings and worlds. After His Ascension when He was free to do so, He sojourned and investigated the various spheres because He had been extremely interested to know what was there. And so He had a wonderful time.

He made the Ascension into blazing light there on Mount Shasta that day. He, as well as Godfré Ray King, had registered that morning with the Forest ranger as is the requirement when one goes beyond a certain height. That evening Godfré checked out but there was no account of David Lloyd. Some years later several persons from Florida went to Mount Shasta for their vacation. They got acquainted with the Forest ranger in that locality, and learned from him that they had had a searching party out searching for David Lloyd for three weeks but never found any trace of Him.

He offered to give assistance to the younger generation.

He gave His first dictation March 24, 1937. He is sponsoring Australia.

SAINT PATRICK

Saint Patrick the apostle or patron saint of Ireland, is said to have been born in Scotland; and became a monk in France. A vision led him to go to Ireland about the year four hundred thirty-two with the idea to convert the pagan Irish. His endeavors were very successful and he established a number of schools and monasteries. It is said his mission lasted about forty years.

He was not an incarnation of Lord Maitreya but was overshadowed by Him as Jesus was, that is, he was enfolded in Lord Maitreya's Cosmic Flame which enabled him to perform the various miracles (so-called), attributed to him, particularly the expulsion of all venomous creatures from Ireland.

Saint Patrick stood many hours, even through the rain, persistently calling and commanding the assistance of the powers of God for the people's benefit, until finally the Cosmic Being Victory released the action, which made him victorious.

He is now an Ascended Being.

March seventeenth is recognized as Saint Patrick's Day.

FUN WEY

Fun Wey as a small child in China was saved from death by the Ascended Master Eriel and brought to His Retreat.

He is of the Elemental evolution, went through physical embodiments, and attained the Ascension there in Eriel's Retreat. He gave complete obedience and gained His victory quickly under the direction and in the radiation of the Master Eriel. He had given much service over a long period of time.

His special qualities are joy and happiness and His activity is to serve.

Fun Wey is over six feet tall and very slender. His keynote is "In a Country Garden". His electronic pattern is that of lily of the valley.

CARDINAL BONZANO

Cardinal Bonzano attended the Eucharistic Congress in Chicago (June 1926), this is when his Ascension really began. He is ascended now. He completed the Ascension in November, nineteen twenty-seven, under the New Dispensation, which acted for Him, although it had not yet been made known to the students.

He was (Father) Jacques Marquette the French missionary, in a former embodiment.

He had rendered great service in many embodiments and this enabled Him to attain His victory at the close of this lifetime.

GODFRÉ RAY KING

The inner meaning of Godfré Ray King is, "God frees by the power of light and becomes king." He was known in the outer world by the name of Guy W. Ballard. He was the channel in human form that the Ascended Master Saint Germain prepared and used to bring forth this instruction to mankind. He was the open door through which the Ascended Masters could work in the physical realm. The Ascended Masters gave the information and instruction through him to the students. Thus they learned how to cooperate with the Ascended Masters and thereby handle conditions of world wide as well as of cosmic import. Godfré was the Messenger and under the direct directions of the Ascended Master Saint Germain. He was one of the sons of the King (Saint Germain) in that civilization seventy thousand years ago. He was the Roman Centurion AEmilius in Jesus' time and offered Him assistance. Jesus refused, knowing the mission He Himself had to fulfill; also knowing the service Godfré would render in this future day, in bringing forth this instruction. The Roman Centurion later became Procurator (Governor) of the Island of Britain. He and Adina were the first to entertain Saint Paul, the Apostle, on his mission there to proclaim the teaching of Jesus the Christ.

It was given out that he was Richard the Lionhearted (1157-1199), and George Washington (1732-1799) in previous embodiments.

His predominant quality is "Obedience". He is now also referred to as the God Obedience. His Cosmic Name is Obedience. On the inner He is known as Godfré.

It is only because of that obedience that so much was accomplished. That is, he gave illumined obedience.

With most people, that is with the masses who give obedience, it is blind obedience. Usually they obey the domination of some strong person. Illumined obedience is when one gives obedience to the flame in the heart through understanding instead of the dictates of another.

He is also referred to as the "Great Physician". During his ministry on Earth (in a period of five years), more than twenty thousand instantaneous healings took place at his calls. Many so-called miracles took place through him as well as precipitation at various times. He manifested Christ Consciousness through the outer form. He was the focus in the physical realm for the Christ action.

To outer appearance he looked like other men in physical form. Yet he was different. His inner bodies (vehicles) had been purified. This enabled the powers of light to flow through freely. That was the state in which he rendered (public) service for the last three years of his life in physical form. In nineteen thirty-six he had rendered sufficient service to completely balance his account with life and could have ascended then, but he chose of his own free will to stay and be the contact and channel through whom the Ascended Ones could work, as well as reach mankind.

At the end of nineteen thirty-nine he left the world of form and completed his Ascension New Year's Eve under the New Dispensation.

Before he went to Mount Shasta and then had those experiences, he was engaged in some mining business. All odds seemed to be against him. One day in Los An-

geles, he had been up to the office of some mining engi-
neers and things were very unfavorable, he was walking
along the street on Broadway when all of a sudden he
turned and emphatically said: "You have scared me for
the last time. You have no power!" He was really speak-
ing to that limiting force, which was his human creation.
From then on things began to turn for the better. Shortly
after that he was called on a government position at
Mount Shasta where he later met the Ascended Master
Saint Germain in a visible tangible body. After that
he had those experiences which are recorded as well as
some that are not recorded.

The Masters told us some years later that had he not
taken his stand against the human that day there in
Los Angeles, that ten minutes later it would have been
too late. That was a cosmic moment and had he not
acted in accordance with it he could not have become
the channel for this instruction, and it could not have
been given.

About ten years later as we stood, presumably on that
same spot, we were aware of a definite current of energy
there. And on the sidewalk there had been placed a
symbol which consisted of three plumes. The shopkeeper
had some of this higher knowledge and had placed it
there. Of course he was not aware of what had taken
place at that spot.

He was taken by the Master Saint Germain into some
of the Retreats to experience these things first hand so
he would have the full conscious awareness of the powers

and inner actions of the Law. He witnessed two Ascensions in the Cave of Symbols.

He had these experiences in a body created of pure light by Saint Germain, for him to function in. This body had no imperfections in it. It was as visible and tangible as any physical body and he paid his fare on the steamboat and taxi cabs et cetera, as did Rex, Bob, Nada and Pearl who were in their own physical bodies.

To have such experiences so raises the vibratory action of the physical and inner bodies that one would soon go through into the Ascension. Therefore the great Law permitted this body to be provided for him. His own physical body was in an apartment in Denver Colorado, at the time. He would step out of it and go in this other body with the others of the party or wherever directed to go. He would return into his own physical body ever so often (once in twenty-four hours) and take care of it. When he was away from it it was as in a deep sleep.

If he had had those experiences in his physical body it would have so raised and perfected it that he too would have ascended. This way it enabled him to witness and be a part of these great activities and in that way draw the substance and *feeling* into his outer consciousness and thus remain here to give and relay this knowledge, instruction and *feeling* to the students and mankind at the public classes all over the United States as well as through the books.

He said he could do many things while in that other body which He could not do in his own. He could drive an automobile which he never did in his life in his physical body. The Three-fold Flame stood on his palm without any ill effects.

While having those experiences he was made a member of the Great White Brotherhood as were also others in that party. That was the first time unascended beings were admitted to the Retreat before they were members.

When he came back home after having those experiences his light was greatly intensified. As he again contacted and lived in the outer world his light began to gradually diminish, to recede to some extent. This was noticed and observed by a student, and it goes to show what the power of the attention will do, and how important it is.

He is now six feet eight inches in height. His favorite flower is the (violet) lilac.

NADA

There are several Ascended Lady Masters known to us by the name of Nada. There is the One Who made the Ascension long ago, Mrs. Rayborn and Her daughter and a child who made the Ascension at about ten years of age. This child was a student of this instruction and made the Ascension in August 1942 in Chicago, Illinois.

MRS. NADA RAYBORN

Mrs. Rayborn had secret instruction by the Masters. When She passed on in the earlier part of this century, She was given the assistance and attained the Ascension.

The family did not know this until years later, but had they looked into the casket just before burial they would have found no body there.

She has the particular ability to radiate the feeling of the attainment of the Ascension to students. She is also a great singer.

MR. DANIEL RAYBORN

Mr. Rayborn, with his wife, Nada, and two children, Rex and Nada, lived on a ranch on the slopes of the Rocky Mountains. They also own a mine of great wealth. He was a very good business man and through his radiation of natural kindness and brotherhood, maintained harmony amongst his men. This was very unusual, especially at a mine. The Law permitted the Ascended Masters, because of the harmony maintained amongst the men, to transmute a certain portion of their human creation at a particular time. This was done unbeknown to the men.

He will give assistance in business matters to students at their call.

He attained the Ascension with the assistance of the Atomic Accelerator in the Cave of Symbols. (The date given was July 1932.)

REX AND NADA RAYBORN—BOB AND
PEARL SINGLETON

These four young people grew up and were educated here in the United States. When in college they were given special training under the direction of their Master Saint Germain.

They were in the party with Godfré, went to the Far East and were given training in the Retreats, particularly in the Cave of Light. This enabled them to completely purify their four lower bodies. Therefore, they could release great power by the wielding of light rays. They gave tremendous protection and rendered very great service for the blessing of mankind in those perfected bodies just before their Ascension. The vibratory action of their bodies was accentuated and raised to a degree where they would no longer register discord. This enabled them to draw great power and render tremendous service which has not yet been made known to the outer world.

They, not yet being ascended, by retaining the physical bodies, gave them a connection with the physical world which is no longer apparent after the Ascension. This enabled them to render certain service which the great Law would not permit an Ascended Being to do.

After rendering certain service in those perfected bodies they completed the Ascension in about March nineteen thirty-three. Now from the Ascended State Their special activity is to assist the younger generation.

Rex still over-saw the management of their ranch and mine after the Ascension. He would occasionally return in the visible, tangible body to tend to things. The men there of course did not know that He was Ascended.

Rex is on the gold ray.

A short time after Her Ascension Nada had taken on the powerful qualities of the Lady Master Nada Who had ascended so long ago.

She is also on the pink ray.

Bob had very great enthusiasm and could pour forth a mighty radiance. His color is blue.

Pearl represents purity and Her color is white.

The four children entered the Retreat before they were made members of the Great White Brotherhood. That was never permitted before.

THE ANGELIC HOSTS

Angels, Cherubim, Seraphim, Angel Devas and Archangels make up the Angelic Hosts.

They have names; They are Beings with feelings and have a purpose in life. As They serve silently They give of Their life—qualified energies; They radiate some particular quality.

They are wholly pure and perfect Beings. They grow in size and capacity through service to which They are assigned, and through love from those whom They serve, whether ascended or unascended. They have golden or light colored hair and are extremely beautiful. In nature They are one-pointed, Beings of one particular virtue— one quality or activity; while man is twelve-fold in nature.

Angels are impregnated with a certain quality in the great spheres or auras of Ascended Masters and Divine Beings and then radiate that to wherever They are sent. They need not labor, but They just shine. Angels are sent to serve mankind and must obey. They obey instantly the directions or commands of the Masters. They are intelligent Beings of love and do not reason, but willingly and joyously give obedience; they respond immediately to a call.

Their service is not only to give or implant a certain specific quality in the feelings of someone requiring it, but They will and do expand the good qualities and activities already within mankind.

Angels are primarily protectors; They radiate and amplify God qualities. Their response or action is in connection with the emotional world of mankind, while the elementals respond to thought formed by the mind.

The Angels grow and develop mainly through radiation. They learn the control of energy. They can become Cherubim, Seraphim, Archangels and greater Beings.

Angels deal with energy and its actions. When seen with the inner sight, They appear more in streams and circles of energies (forces) than in actual form. Angels are invoked and created by Cosmic Beings in any number, whatsoever is required. There are countless numbers of Angels who serve at inner levels who never contact the world of form. Every Ascended Master and Cosmic Being has many Angels serving with Him. There are Angels of all the various qualities and activities. There are Angels of Light, Divine Love, Peace, Healing, Wisdom, Freedom, Victory, Music, Purity, Joy, Justice, Mercy, Obedience, Wealth, Angels of the Flame, Angels of the Three-fold Flame, Angels of the Violet Flame, Blue Flame, Pink

Flame, and of each specific Flame, Angels of White Fire, Angels of Blue Lightning, Angels of the Flaming Sword, et cetera. They usually form the court and attend an Ascended Being. Many render service in the physical realm with mankind. Their service is to guard energy, and to hold radiation. The Angel wraps Its own divine love about the stream of energy so that no destructive force can use that energy. In connection with mankind They are to project a certain quality (whichever is theirs) and hold it to assist persons or conditions. They carry the virtue of the Being Who created Them.

When one calls forth the Healing Flame of the Cosmic Christ an Angel can stand beside him and direct the Flame until the physical body can stand that vibratory action, then it can be drawn through himself.

Some of the Angelic Host have incarnated—have taken physical embodiment and live as human beings, seldom known to themselves. They have taken on human qualities as has the rest of mankind. They can be called "fallen angels", as the saying goes. When they take on embodiment they come under the inner and outer laws of mankind, becoming one with that kingdom. In other words they are transferred from the Angelic kingdom to that of mankind; and are to develop in nature likewise.

Unlike the beings of the elements (who are also created by Ascended and Cosmic Beings), they do not take on and express human qualities when serving mankind. However, when discord is too great they may be unable to withstand the strain and hold their virtue, thus becom-

ing deficient. Then they are recharged by some great
Being or go back to the Sun for regeneration.

The Cherubim are larger in size than the Angels. Their
nature is to absorb the virtues of whatever realm They
go to, or from the Presence of Divine Beings. Their main
service is to guard energy. They stand guard and protect
great streams of energy drawn by Ascended and Cosmic
Beings, and radiate that quality. They serve mostly at
inner levels and not so much with mankind; however
this action has somewhat changed within the past several
years. They may go into the radiation of any of the
Temples in any one of the seven spheres or go within
the belt around the Sun, there be imbued with God qualities and then bring that virtue and radiate it out. They
are also a part of the court of Great Beings as They move
through the universe.

Cherubim can become Devas. Those Who have guarded
focuses of energy for long periods of time become Silent
Watchers of planets, systems and galaxies.

Seraphim are large in stature, from six to fourteen feet
tall, very slight of form, and have great strength. They
come from the Heart of God, the Central Sun, as do the
Cherubim. They move in V-formation in groups of seven.
The Seraphim are the guardians of the energies of great
Beings in Their cosmic creations. Many of Them abide
in the Realm of Bey. They have only in recent years
come into the atmosphere of Earth to serve.

The Seraphim are the largest in size; They manifest in
action next higher to the Cherubim. Their service is in

greater capacity than the Cherubim; They handle more extreme rays—energy; They guard the most intense powers of the Sacred Fire. They serve almost entirely at inner levels, seldom in connection with mankind. They precede Great Beings in Their service about the universe. Ministration is Their service. They are the messengers of the Suns of the systems.

There are Angel Devas and Angels over churches, hospitals and various activities of mankind. They guard Temples, cities, states, nations and world activities.

There are some of the Devas Who can make Themselves visible on Earth, Who carry a wand and produce whatever They call for.

The Angels' activity is the power to vitalize form through feeling. The Elemental's activity is the power to create form.

Elementals become Builders of Form; some become Devas also great Beings Who guard mountains, Elohim or Silent Watchers (of a planet, solar system or galaxy).

Their nature is to imitate; that is how they grow and develop. Man through directed and controlled thought in cooperation with controlled feeling (these two representing the elemental and angelic kingdoms), will have mastery and thus connect the three kingdoms. Then will the Angels and Elementals again work in cooperation with mankind. Elemental life is commanded to obey the Threefold Flame, by Cosmic Law.

The Spirit of Christmas is a feeling of forgiveness, good will, and impersonal love. That is due to the radiation, the outpouring from the Heavenly Hosts. There is also the Spirit of Christmas Who is a real Being, an Angel Deva, Whose name is Mary. She is guardian of the Christian Dispensation, as Micah is for the Jewish Dispensation.

There is the Angel Deva of the Jade Temple Whose service is as guardian of this original instruction and activity of the Ascended Masters. This Being's color is primarily green.

The Being Who guards the later instruction and activity of the Ascended Masters is the Cherub Lovelee. Her color is mainly green.

The Spirit of the Ascension Flame is a living, real and intelligent Being, Who is the intelligence within that Flame. This Being is the embodiment of the Ascension Flame and Its activity; Who holds within the atmosphere of Earth that action of the Sacred Fire in cosmic capacity.

Within the electrons that constitute the bodies of an individual and the light flowing into him from his Source, is every (potential) quality and activity of the Sacred Fire. This Being when summoned by one's life, can draw forth the dormant quality of the Ascension Flame and activate it within the electrons and merge it with the cosmic activity of the Ascension Flame. This quickens or accelerates the vibratory action of every atom in the four lower bodies; when that action expands to the point where it connects and merges completely with the cosmic action of the Spirit of the Ascension Flame they become one and

DIVINE BEINGS, OFFICES and ACTIVITIES

This diagram shows the principal actions and positions of the Planetary Hierarchy, and that portion of the Solar Hierarchy directly pertaining to the Earth. The circles indicate potent offices, and the lines indicate direct currents of energy and the connections between them.

January 1, 1956, Lord Gautama Buddha became "Lord of the World," and the former One, Lord Sanat Kumara took the position of Regent (until the Earth's crisis is passed). Lord Maitreya now holds the office of The Buddha, but still oversees His former position of World Teacher.

The Manu of the fourth root race is Lord Himalaya, also known as Lord Chakshusha. The Manu of the fifth root race is Lord Vaivasvata. The Manu of the sixth root race is Lord Meru. The Manu of the seventh root race is the Cosmic Being, the Divine Director.

The Ascended Masters, Kuthumi and Jesus now hold the office of World Teacher (the first time that there have been two).

Ascended Lady Master Nada has become Chohan of the Sixth Ray and the Ascended Master Lanto has assumed Chohanship of the Second Ray.

May 1, 1954, the Ascended Master Saint Germain became Cosmic Authority of the New Cycle of two thousand years. The Sixth Ray, predominating for the last two thousand years, was transferred to the Seventh Ray.

this results in the Ascension of the individual; before that one can have its action in degrees.

This Being's keynote is "Aloha Oe".

A similar action can take place with the Flames of Transmutation, Resurrection, Illumination, et cetera.

CHOHANS—RAYS

Chohan means "Lord"—"Law," Maha means great.

A Chohan is the Lord of one of the seven Rays, He is the Law of that Ray to the Earth.

An Ascended Being is Master of all seven rays before He becomes Chohan of any one ray; therefore a Chohan is Master on all seven rays but predominates on one. He may or can even be Chohan of some other ray than the ray He is on, that is His natural ray.

The Chohans' action is to serve the souls and life-streams of embodied mankind, as well as those at inner levels.

The Chohan of a new cycle enters the Great Silence before He starts a new endeavor, to find the best way of presenting the Law at that time; so that it will be of a vibratory action that reaches the conscious mind of mankind. The Chohan of the two thousand year cycle is the channel through which the activity, education, radiation and designed religion flows.

The purpose of the Ascended Masters' instruction is to bring a balance between the consciousnesses of the East and the West, at this time. That is particularly the work of the Chohans.

The Chohans of the seven Rays are the messengers of the Seven Elohim from the Central Sun to the Earth. The Seven Archangels were the first Chohans of the rays for the Earth. The Chohans work more closely with mankind than these other Beings. The Chohans on the rays, three to seven, have always been under the Lord Maha Chohan, but in recent years the first two have also been placed directly under the Maha Chohan.

The Chohan of the First Ray is Lieutenant of the Manu. The Chohan of the Second Ray can become the Cosmic Christ and World Teacher. The Chohan of the Third Ray can become the Maha Chohan.

Archangel Zadkiel was the first Chohan on the Seventh Ray; Lord Sanat Kumara, Lord Gautama and Kwan Yin have been Chohans on this ray and now Saint Germain is the Chohan of this ray.

Chohans are strict because and according to the quality or activity each One represents; it must be so. Morya holds to the strictest disciplines of the Chohans; Serapis comes second.

Rays. An abstract principle is made manifest by a light ray.

There is life or actions of life below and above the visible radiation or vibrations. That of the slower frequency (below) is known as the infra ray and the more rapid frequency (above) as the ultra-violet ray.

All of the gifts, benefits, activities and progress of the race enter the individuals' worlds and experiences on the seven rays.

The seven rays represent the diversified activities of cosmic service from the God-Parents, the Sun. The seven rays are life manifest in seven different ways, seven phases or activities of development. These rays are directed to the planet through the Seven Elohim, Archangels and Chohans.

The First, Second and Third Rays represent the Three-fold action of the Godhead; they represent the inner action. The other four rays represent the outer action, that is, that of the etheric, mental, emotional and physical planes. The Fourth Ray corresponds with the etheric, the bridge between the inner and outer.

The colors of the seven rays as herein explained may seem to differ from other literature. The information of the specific colors of the rays was not permitted under the occult (old) law, but was given in blinds, and the exact color was left for the individual to discover, unless one was familiar with the blinds used. Now that the action of the Cosmic Law has been changed and the Cosmic Light has taken sufficient command, mysticism and abstractions no longer prevail as before, but definite and more complete information is permitted.

Jewels are condensed light. They are a (most) pure concentrate of fire.

The **First Ray** represents the Will of God. The very first activity of an individual is to will (to do something) what to do. It is to make the decision. It is to draw life for a purpose. The ideas come forth on this ray from the heart of creation. A tendency, when not wholly construc-tive, of the first ray, is hard feelings, which come from looking to appearances instead of to the I AM Presence and powers of God.

The activity and qualities of the first ray are protection, power, faith and initiative. Executives and rulers come under this, as do governmental activities and affairs.

The color is blue; the jewel is the diamond or sapphire. The Chohan is Morya.

The **Second Ray,** is that of illumination, the capacity to cognize, enlightenment, perception, comprehension and education; the giving of the instruction which is required to become master of energy. Here is worked (or figured) out, planned, how to utilize and make ideas practical. The second ray activity draws forth the plan in humility and finds out how best to do it. Here one learns the law of cause and effect, and the divine scheme of things is revealed—the plan of the Hierarchy and how individuals fit into the divine plan. This is the ray of directing intelligence, discrimination, discretion and direction in the use of one's life.

The qualities or activities are understanding, wisdom (through love), the Christ activity. Teachers, educators and students come under this ray. The youth come under this Chohan.

The color is yellow; the jewel is the topaz. The Chohan has been Kuthumi, but Ascended Master Lanto is assuming the office at this time.

The **Third Ray** is that of tolerance, divine love, adoration, forbearance, spirit of good will, unity, brotherhood, tact, culture; it is the cohesive power. The particular activity of the third ray is to harmonize, raise, purify and

The color is (bright) green; the jewel is the emerald. The Chohan is Hilarion.

This **Sixth Ray** cycle of two thousand years now closing was designed to supersede the scientific action of exactitude (the Mosaic law) by the activity of devotion, forgiveness, mercy and grace.

Spiritual nourishment comes under this ray, the radiating of spiritual vitality to all life as well as to mankind. It is the ray of devotional worship and faith in God. It is the ray of peace, tranquility, healing, ministration, and the assistance to harmonize, to re-establish and hold—harmony. It is the expansion of service and the sustaining power. It is the action of enfolding peace of the Elohim of Peace, to hold sustained harmony which makes manifestations permanent.

The qualities or activities are devotion, ministration and peace.

Ministers, priests and healers come under this ray.

The color is ruby (deep pink) or gold; the jewel is the ruby. Lady Master Nada has accepted the Chohanship of this ray for the time being, releasing the beloved Jesus Who has held this position since His Ascension.

The **Seventh Ray** is the ray of Freedom. The seventh, the Violet Ray, has now become active on the Earth. It is the ceremonial ray, the ray of conscious invocation, by which the quality of energy is changed. It will be the predominant vibration for the Earth for the next two thousand year cycle. Its action is that of purification and redemption; it is the ray of sublimation and transmutation and also that of magnetization. The Violet Flame, the Flame or transmutation, is the divine alchemy which resurrects and perfects energy. This provides the opportunity to make things right. The ceremonial ray enables the individual to consciously change the quality of energy at will, in himself and the world about him. This ray also gives opportunity to render cosmic service along with individual development.

The activity of the seventh ray is transubstantiation, conscious transmutation which results in divine alchemy. It is a science; a drawing of energy into a form or condition to change it. This is done through invocation or/and visualizing, thus focusing the energy, and when the intelligence in that energy acts, substance changes. Individuals are ordinarily unconsciously changing the pure energy they receive from the Presence with imperfect qualities; the seventh ray activity is to change and qualify energy consciously, into perfection again.

The Violet Flame is the Flame of forgiveness; it is the activity or power used in etherealization. This action is used on other planets to transmute and return the substance back to the universal of anything which has fulfilled its service and is of no further use. This includes their (physical) bodies at the end of a lifetime, a life service. Etherealization is simply releasing the electrons back into the unformed, ready to be used again in composing new forms or other manifestations. The Violet Flame is used in all higher realms. It is used by divine and

Ascended Beings to etherealize whatever has come forth or been drawn forth in any realm that was not used or utilized as well as all that which has been utilized and has completed its service; thereby returning the substance back into that particular realm for use again. Life is very conservative.

The action of the seventh ray is not only that of the Transmuting Violet Flame for purification, but in it is also the action to invoke or magnetize and radiate. This is its use on other planets where it is not required for purification as is the case with Earth.

The activity of the seventh ray is to draw the Sacred Fire through the power of invocation; through the invocative power of thought, feeling and spoken word.

The Three-fold Flame is the magnet within an individual that draws primal life from his Source—God. He, through thought and feeling, colors or qualifies that primal life and what he is today is the result of that, thus he creates his own aura—his sphere of influence.

It is known that rapid vibrations rise; they are drawn to the realms of light where the frequency is rapid. While the slower or heavier ones descend or sink and stay in the atmosphere of Earth. That is why the perfection from the realms of light must be drawn down here and in order to do that there must be a magnetic center, a magnetization by which it is drawn and then radiated out. This is done through individuals and through groups. This is a service of the seventh ray.

The primary action of this ray is invocation. The pow-

ers must be invoked by someone abiding in the realm
which is to be blessed. That is a requirement of the great
Law governing the universe, otherwise the Ascended Masters could have perfected this world long ago. Jesus went
into the psychic realm (hell) in co-operation with the
Law during that period (three days) in the tomb, to invoke the powers into that realm. People must use the
power of invocation to invoke the Sacred Fire and direct
and dispense it through themselves into the atmosphere
to bring about the blessings required here.

The difference between the use of the powers of invocation of the past and now is, in the past they were used
(through prayer or some manner) mainly to nourish mankind; now they are being used for the freedom of all life,
mankind, elemental life, and the Earth itself. The power
of invocation is effectual at inner levels too, changing
conditions there, as well as on Earth. Lifestreams are being blessed there before coming into embodiment again,
and many thousands are being released from the necessity
of re-embodiment. They have the opportunity to complete
the Ascension in the inner spheres through training and
preparation in the Ascension Temples which have been
called forth and built for that purpose. These actions are
affecting all planetary evolutions. The redemption of mankind and the Earth is through the power of invocation.
This service anyone may render through the art of decreeing and the willingness so to do impersonally for the
good of the whole, to bless all life.

The service of the seventh ray is to teach mankind how

to draw, qualify and radiate energy, which is *Life,* in a manner that will increase the glory of the planet and all evolutions on it. An action of the seventh ray in the new age is that of a brotherhood among men, as well as the conscious and tangible association between angels, men and the elementals.

The ceremonial ray is expressed through ordered service; it becomes a ritual of daily life. It is the action of rhythmic invocation and radiation. Rhythm comes under this ray, the returning to one's activity of service rhythmically; the rhythmic feeding, at or near the same hour daily.

The activities and qualities of the seventh ray are, rhythmic application, transmutation, invocation, magnetization, radiation and ordered service, diplomacy, courtesy, refinement and culture.

The gentlemen and diplomats come under this ray.

The color is violet and purple; the jewel is the amethyst. The Chohan is the Ascended Master Saint Germain, Who is also the authority for the new age.

FLAME

Wisdom is not only having knowledge, but the right use of it.

The Sacred Fire—what is this which is so little understood by mankind? The various Flames of the Sacred Fire are concentrated energy, which are specifically qualified by some intelligent Being.

All know what a powerful activity physical fire is; how

it can transform and transmute substance, into what? It is returned back into universal substance, into light substance.

Fire is such a blessing to mankind. It transmutes the rubbage and waste, the things no longer of use to them; by it heat is produced through various methods for warmth when required, which is such a great comfort and blessing. However, physical fire will also destroy, as it is an impersonal activity and just acts wherever it is.

Fire is the outer or physical activity of the Sacred Fire, which is an inner activity not ordinarily seen with the physical sight; but can be seen with the All-seeing Eye or inner sight, by those who have that faculty developed. Fire is a fourth dimensional activity.

Sacred Fire means the inner action of the fire element.

Each one's self-conscious being, the real identity, is inately *flame*.

Life, in outer expression, is but qualified life.

There are the three activities of the fire element; it transmutes, creates and sustains. In these activities are both the masculine and feminine elements; which, when combined, produce the action.

Flame in the atmosphere of Earth has the tendency to rise, that is, its natural action is to rise and go back into its own realm which is of a more rapid vibratory action and of a similar frequency. Therefore, recognition, love and invocation are necessary to have the Flames and their actions here.

These various Flames of the Sacred Fire are *real*, a

mighty current of energy, and not just abstract or ephemeral. The action of a Ray or Flame (as well as a quality) always has a (conscious) directing intelligence, a Being behind it, and it is not just some abstract idea. The quality, virtue or activity which a Flame represents is anchored within it.

The very center of all Flames is white.

The Three-fold Flame in the heart magnetizes primal life and the individual has the liberty to qualify it as he will through the action of *free will*.

The Three-fold Flame (a balance of love, wisdom and power), which was established by Sanat Kumara at Shamballa when He came to Earth connected with and sustained the Three-fold Flame in the heart of every lifestream by a tiny thread of light, otherwise the Christ Self would have withdrawn entirely.

The use of fire was practically forgotten by the masses before the coming of Sanat Kumara and the Lords of Flame from Venus. It was known only to the spiritual lifestreams who retained the knowledge of the Sacred Fire, who had not ignored and forgotten the immortal flame in their hearts. After the coming of Sanat Kumara, there was established the Sacred Fire at Shamballa, visible to the people. The people went once a year to the City of White—Shamballa, built a pile of (sandal) wood; above Sanat Kumara's chair was a star. When He would come the star would flash and He appeared. He extended His hand and flame flashed, lighting the wood. The people took a piece of the wood aflame into their homes; it burned around the three or four inch piece of wood, which lasted for a year. That was the flame from Sanat Kumara's lifestream, He sustained it for a year, then it was renewed and intensified once a year. This tiny flame kept all discord consumed in the homes. There were no crimes, armies or navies. This lasted for thousands of years.

One can call forth and establish the Three-fold Flame in his home. He need not see it with the physical sight. The Three-fold Flame is an action of life-giving essence. When establishing a focus of the Sacred Fire in an undisturbed place in the home or a sanctuary, use the Three-fold Flame. Lord Sanat Kumara, Lord Gautama in His place now, the Goddess of Justice and the Cosmic Being Pelleur (Pelleur in the center of the Earth), form a three-fold action; Faith, Hope and Charity, form another. The Divine Director, the Grand Teton Retreat, the Brothers of the Golden Robe, Godfre' and Others govern the activities of the Three-fold Flame to the Earth. (It is well to call to Lord Gautama, the new Lord of the World instead of Sanat Kumara so as to leave Him free since He is going to be on Venus.)

The power of the Three times Three means the actions of three Three-fold Flames. One such action is the Three-fold Flame in one's heart with that in the heart of his Christ Self and I AM Presence. Another such action of each lifestream is the Cosmic Action of the two I AM Presences (of the Twin Rays) and the God-Flame. Three

Ascended Masters or Cosmic Beings may for some specific service or accomplishment form the action of the Three-fold Flame; One representing Love, One Wisdom and the Other Power. This forms an action of the Power of the Three times Three.

The **Seven-fold Flame** on the forehead is a Flame (the quality) from the heart of each of the Seven Elohim anchored there in every lifestream, embodied or disembodied. These seven Flames compose the Seven-fold Flame, placed in order of the rays from left (side) to right. A Master can readily tell what ray an individual is on by the predominance of that ray in this Seven-fold Flame on the forehead. The Three-fold Flame in the heart is from the Presence, the Seven-fold Flame of the Seven Elohim on the forehead is a balancing power to assist that Flame. The action of the Three-fold Flame of Cosmic Beings, Faith, Hope and Charity anchored around the heart of each lifestream is similar to the Flame on the forehead.

The potential power of any flame is within the Three-fold Flame in the heart, comfort, healing, peace, truth, transmutation, et cetera. Within that flame is the power; through that tiny flame is generated enough energy—power to make even a husky man function. That should be proof that the Flame need not be as large as the discord in order to handle it. A similar action is that of a wire carrying the electricity to light a building or even a city, is not as large as the building or city; yet enough power flows through.

An action (of the flame) that can be used is to draw the discord of each body into the Flame in the heart and command it to be transmuted.

One can also visualize and feel a large Three-fold Flame around the physical body. It is like three ostrich plumes or pampas grass, from beneath the feet extending to a foot or so above the head, with the blue plume at the left side, slightly to the back, the gold one in front and the pink one at the right, meeting the blue one at the center back.

Another action one can use is to draw the action of the Seven-fold Flame of the Elohim around oneself, through visualization. When one can visualize and get the *feeling* of this, it is a tremendous drawing power of the release of the accumulated good in the Causal Body. In the beginning to visualize it one can take the mental picture of standing on a disc (like a phonograph record) a foot or two in diameter, see that white in color; now make it a pillar extending to above the head. Then outside around that see a blue disc a foot wide; next one yellow in color; outside around that a disc or circle, pink in color; around that one crystal or white; next one bright green; the next one ruby (or gold) ; and the final one violet or purple. As one holds a good clear mental picture see each one becoming a flame blazing up, forming a pillar of these various colors. Later on it can be pictured and formed into a sphere which in reality it is in its natural state.

The **Blue Flame** is greatly concentrated energy and

very powerful, therefore must always be used in deep love.

The **Sword of Blue Flame** can be struck into very destructive or dense conditions and activities at inner levels by the I AM Presence, the Christ Self and Divine Beings, by which it can be shattered and transmuted.

The **Cross of Blue Flame** can be used for protection, also to silence and hold inactive destructive forces.

The **Spiral Blue Flame** can be used to encircle destructive forces, cores and causes and pull out and transmute them.

The **Cosmic Blue Lightning** is concentrated energy of the fire element. It is an action of divine love and is used to purify the dense substance. The use of the Cosmic Blue Lightning of divine love and purity is the only way or means to purify some of the density of earth substance. It has a consuming and trasmuting power but its main action is to shatter and loosen dense and hard substance. Then it can be more easily and quickly handled by the Transmuting Violet Flame.

The Lords of Blue Flame govern the activity of electricity to Earth.

The **Flame of Fearlessness** can be called forth to consume, transmute all fear and doubt. The action of the Flame may be gold with a pink center, and outer edge blue; gold with violet radiance or gold with pink like changeable silk. The Cosmic Being Ray-O-Light is the Director of this Flame.

The quality and power of the Sacred Fire is within

every electron, although latent it can be activated on an instant. One can focus the attention on the Three-fold Flame, the Immortal Flame within the heart and with the (seeing) power of that Flame see every organ ful-filling its perfect function and plan, accepting eternal life instead of old age and death. See the central cores of the atoms expand and those electrons swinging, swirl-ing around them throwing off the shadows, which are then transmuted in the Flame. This will raise the vibra-tory action of the four lower bodies. The Flames on Le-muria and Atlantis, manifesting in the temples were of the various qualities necessary to attainment and com-plete freedom of each individual on Earth. Therefore, before the sinking of these continents a portion of the Flame of the various qualities was taken from the tem-ples by a priest of that temple and with chosen associates they started out for places of safety, under inner direc-tion; so that they might be preserved for the future. Thus a connection of that particular quality—flame would be sustained on Earth. Some of the individuals entrusted with that Flame failed to arrive at their destination within the appointed time; but those who did reach their destina-tions with those Flames have been sustained and are great foci of light today.

Each individualization when projected forth contains within it a specific pattern or design which forms the permanent atom, and qualifies all energy flowing through that lifestream with that pattern. There is also a specific fragrance, and a Sacred Tone, a certain vibratory action around which is formed a melody or piece of music.

There is an action of the element of fire—the Sacred Fire within each of the other three elements (air, water, earth). These three form the cup or receptacle into which the flame can descend into the three dimensional plane.

The squaring of the circle is balanced action of the four elements, which will bring the Earth back into perfection. Fire, air and water form the trinity of action. When these three elements act wholly constructively, perfection is made manifest in the earth element on Earth, thus squaring the circle. Life is a circle. To square all in the circle, one must square himself with Life, by balancing himself, which represents the squaring of the circle. This can be produced by the use of the Sacred Fire.

THE TWELVE VIRTUES

The qualities, virtues or actions the planets require in their evolution or progress are provided by the Twelve Cosmic Qualities of the Sun, the twelve-fold nature of the Sun God and Goddess. These form the Electronic Belt around the Sun. Each of these qualities is under the direction of a Cosmic Being (with the Twin Ray), Who offered to take the responsibility of magnetizing and radiating that quality into the universe in rhythmic action. Their relationship to the Sun is for each One to specialize, concentrate and intensify one particular virtue embodied by the Sun God and Goddess, Helios and Vesta, of this system. They absorb those Divine Qualities of the Sun and expand them by Their own Flame and radiate them out into the solar system. They are or act as what might be called step-down transformers for the extremely rapid and intense vibratory action of the Godhead, so that life of lesser development can stand it and be benefited thereby. The Twelve Beings are the guardian Presences of the Twelve Cosmic Virtues around the Sun of the system. Their responsibility and service is to sustain these qualities on the planets of Their system and cultivate them in the consciousnesses of those developing, evolving and progressing thereon. They radiate Their particular quality and keep it alive in the hearts, minds and feelings of the people. These Beings control and direct the expansion of light in mankind and the planet.

The Earth moves through the radiation of one of these qualities every thirty days, approximately. The "Houses" or Signs in astrology refer to these. Originally the "Houses" of the zodiac referred to the Temples of the Twelve Cosmic Beings, in the Electronic Belt around the Sun, from which They pour out the radiation of Their particular virtue. Actually there are only vibrations of good that go forth from these "Houses" and no other influence can be attributed to them, nor other planets or stars. The currents or tides of energy the Earth may pass through at certain conjunctions may and will intensify whatever qualities they contact, evil as well as good.

The inner bodies and centers of the people are nourished by the particular quality of the Sign the Earth is moving through. This is more pronounced and stimulating when one has been born under that Sign. One can by acceptance and recognition absorb more of these qualities and derive much greater benefit. Liberty is one of these qualities.

The Twelve Qualities or Actions were represented by the twelve disciples in Jesus' time.

The Etheric City over the Sahara Desert has held and holds an action of the Twelve Pillars which are an action of the Twelve Realms around the Sun and the Central Sun. These are an action of the Twelve Virtues or Attributes of this galaxy.

We can give recognition to and draw the Twelve Pillars of Light from the Sun through the Etheric City, around us or a particular place.

Music is the universal language, for it, we have a scale of twelve tones, represented on the keyboard by seven white keys (which form a major scale), corresponding to the seven planets of our solar system, also, and more important, it corresponds with the seven Suns which form the galaxy. These came forth into outer manifestation, each creating a system for itself. The five black keys (or half tones not used in a major scale), denote the five Suns out of the twelve which did not come out for manifestation as did the seven. They stayed in, and are going on in creation at inner levels. The seven Suns of our galaxy with the other five were created as planets around our present Central Sun (when It was just a Sun) forming a system. These planets then became Suns.

There were twelve definite actions or qualities in the scheme of creation of that system out of which our Sun developed. It was based on the number *twelve*, whereas our solar system is based on the number *seven*.

CENTERS—CHAKRAS

When one first individualized and said and felt "I AM," he began to magnetize primal life and radiate it forth; from this has come the result of what he is today. Each one is endowed with the power of magnetization (to draw what is desired) and the power of radiation (to radiate, give forth) ; these should be under the conscious control of the individual at all times. He should be a radiating focus of light and power.

The present condition of mankind's bodies is that they are negative, and absorbers, accepting and taking on the qualities about them, instead of being positive and radiating focuses and only accept that which is desired.

The seven centers or chakras (see page 74) are connecting points of the lower bodies one with the other, through which flows life energy. It is through these centers, at these points that the inner energy or force flows from one body to another. The centers are usually described as wheels, that denote action, a turning; however, they are spherical and not flat like a wheel. These centers in the etheric body of the spiritually undeveloped individual are declivities, concave in form, which makes a suction, instead of protrusions and convex, which radiate, vibrate with vital essence and power. It is within these declivities that the sins of man and the various destructive qualities and activities are rooted.

These can be removed with the assistance of the Ascended Ones, particularly the Elohim of Purity and Astrea, Archangel Michael, Those on the seventh ray, Ascended Kwan Yin and Prince Oromasis. One can watch himself and at the first vibratory action of any of these qualities call to the I AM Presence and some Ascended Master, to remove it; it is similar to pulling a rubber suction cap from an object. There is a tendency to unconsciously hold on to them—so LET GO!

These centers should be positive, and radiate the qualities and colors of the seven rays. They should magnetize the qualities and activities from the Seven Elohim, Archangels and Chohans and radiate them out.

The awakening of the kundalini fire under the occult law was dangerous without the assistance of a visible Master. One should not unnecessarily dwell on the lower centers but he can concentrate on the heart, throat and head centers and make them blazing light. The heart center is divine love, pink with gold radiance. The throat, the power center is white light with blue radiance.

The door to the mental world is through the pituitary gland; the solar plexus being the door to the emotional body, from the outer world. The five senses are connections with the world without; touch, taste, smell, hearing and sight; sight being the highest.

CHAKRAS - CENTERS

CHAKRAS	NEGATIVE ASPECT (or Quality)	POSITIVE ASPECT (or Quality)	RAYS	BODIES (Connected with)
Crown	None	Connection with Christ Self, Halo	Second	Christ Self
Forehead	Pride, rebellion, arrogance, intellectual reasoning, doubt	All-Seeing Eye, Concentration, Consecration	Fifth	Mental
Throat	Desire for power, envy, jealousy	Power to create according to God's Will	First	Causal Body
Heart	Lethargy, laziness, sloth, indifference, deficiency	Divine Love, Tolerance, Forbearance	Third	Electronic
Solar Plexus	Covetousness, greed, gluttony, fear, feeling of insecurity	Fearlessness, Generosity, Peace	Sixth	Emotional
Spleen Spinal (base of spine)	Hatred, malice, anger, mild dislike Passion, lust	Power of Invocation Purity	Seventh Fourth	Etheric Physical

RAY	COLOR	ELOHIM Masculine aspect	ELOHIM Feminine aspect	ARCHANGELS Masculine	ARCHANGELS Feminine (Archaii)	CHOHAN
First	Blue	Hercules	Amazon	Michael	Faith	Morya
Second	Yellow	Cassiopea	Minerva	Jophiel	Constance	Lanto
Third	Pink	Orion	Angelica	Chamuel	Charity	Paul, The Venetian
Fourth	White	Elohim of Purity (Clair)	Astrea	Gabriel	Hope	Serapis Bey
Fifth	Green	Vista (Cyclopea)	Crystal	Raphael	Mary	Hilarion
Sixth	Ruby or Gold	Elohim of Peace (Tranquility)	Pacifica	Uriel	Donna Grace	Nada
Seventh	Violet (purple)	Arcturus	Diana	Zadkiel	Amethyst	Saint Germain

RETREATS—FOCI

The Brotherhood of the various Retreats are branches or Orders of the Great White Brotherhood.

The Masters in Their training in Retreats and Monasteries throughout the centuries seldom gave more than one mantram or affirmation to a chela (student) in a lifetime. The reason for this is that the teacher giving instruction is responsible to the great Law for what the student does with it. Then the neophyte had to go to the Master, now the Masters come to us, and even the radiation from the Retreats and Foci of Light is being given to students and it is also radiated around the Earth.

Formerly, it was required of an individual on the Path, under occult law, to enter a Retreat in order to attain mastery and the final goal, the Ascension. The method of development was such that it was not safe to proceed except in a Retreat under the direct supervision of a Master. The neophyte did not have the assistance of the Cosmic Light, the Ascended Masters and Cosmic Beings as now, nor did he have the knowledge and action of his I AM Presence as he can have now. Therefore, he had to work through his own human creation which often resulted in very terrifying experiences. These occult initiations were quite severe, even more so from a mental standpoint than physical. Now, all that has been set aside and the individual gets his initiations in every day living in the outer world, through natural means.

A Retreat is a place, a Focus where the Ascended Masters, unascended Masters and chelas have drawn and focused great light. It is a Focus of light, love, wisdom and power which has been maintained over a long period of time. These Retreats are great centers of outpouring of substance and energy; and they are a similar action to the Earth as the ganglionic centers are to the physical body of man and animal. They are places in the physical world, usually in mountains, and at strategic places on the Earth's surface, unknown and unapproachable to the curious. As mankind became more and more selfish and destructive these Foci of Light had to be drawn into the mountains and secluded or inaccessible places, with a protective "ring-pass-not" about them. Some were destroyed and now remain only in the etheric realm.

The word "retreat" should be used only for such Foci and not for person's secluded places or homes.

The Retreats and Foci through their radiation and actions have held the preservation of mankind and saved them through the centuries from complete degradation.

These Foci each specialize in one or more particular quality or activity which the Brothers and Sisters radiate out through the mental and feeling worlds of mankind. Each one of them contains (consists of) the combined radiation and gifts of all those who served on that particular quality or activity through the ages. These special Flames in the Retreats radiate out the essence and feeling of their particular qualities or activities through the emotional, mental and etheric strata (which are one in all mankind), thereby benefiting all on Earth.

Some of the activities and contents of Retreats in the East have been moved from there to Foci in the West (the Americas).

The Retreats sustain the divine qualities and activities in the lower atmosphere of Earth which makes them more available to those who sincerely desire to progress on the Path of Light, as well as through general radiation to all mankind. The Brotherhood of a Retreat keep the Retreat and render service to mankind and all life. They sustain the Flame of that particular Focus through attention and invocation, or else it would ascend into its own natural realm.

The Cosmic Law is also giving assistance through the action of opening a Retreat each month (from the fifteenth of a month to the fourteenth of the following month), to the consciousnesses of mankind. The Hierarchy started this new action in nineteen fifty-two, by opening a different Retreat every month and of transmitting the Flame from that Retreat around the world. So the Earth, its lower atmosphere and the people are bathed in that Flame, quality and activity (whichever it is for the month), particularly the emotional, mental and etheric bodies; and the animal and nature kingdoms receive the benefit of the radiation as well. The students and all constructive individuals are drawn within the radiance of the Retreat in their inner bodies (most of them while asleep), this helps purify and attune their bodies. They can go there and receive the radiation of that particular virtue or activity, thereby being assisted to develop latent qualities, talents and capacities. The Great White Brotherhood direct Their endeavors through this Focus. Daily instruction is given by the Brothers and Sisters for those coming to the Retreat, and some attend councils which are being held. Some only float around in the atmosphere in a state of somnambulism, but do receive the radiation. This is a concentration and momentum of spiritual nourishment.

The keynote of a Retreat is a melody or a piece of music, the closest we have in the outer world to the music of that Retreat. This music, by playing or listening to it (a rendition that is not jazzed), will assist one to tune in on the vibratory action or quality of the Retreat and it helps to draw the radiation from there.

The **Secret Love Star** is a focus of constructively qualified energy of various virtues. It is a power-house consciously focused by Cosmic Beings as a reservoir of already qualified energy from which the Ascended Masters and Cosmic Beings can draw at any moment when They are required to give assistance and produce certain results for mankind, the Earth or other planets. It can be drawn upon also by students consciously applying the law.

There was an outpouring from this Focus during Jesus' lifetime, in that portion of the Earth, which ceased at the time of His Ascension. This was predominantly an outpouring of divine love, as were also the outpourings from it on previous occasions.

The radiation to Earth from this Star began again in September, nineteen thirty-two. This time it is a balance of love, wisdom and power, covering the entire planet, and shall continue for a long time, at least till the new age is well established.

The fourteen **Etheric Cities** are real cities in the etheric realm, located over seven deserts or continents and over seven large bodies of water. Certain Ascended Masters and Divine Beings and sometimes some unascended beings serve in these Etheric Cities in between embodiments. Light Rays are projected from there to the Earth for specific purposes; such as dissolving epidemics and accumulating destructive forces and also light rays are projected into the consciousness of mankind.

The Etheric City over the Sahara Desert is known as the Golden City; Shamballa is over the Gobi Desert; there is one over the Arizona Desert (the action of which covers five States, namely: Arizona, New Mexico, California, Nevada and Utah) ; there is one over the Desert in Brazil; and one over Glastonbury, England.

Ascended Masters and Beings work from these Cities and give assistance to mankind, in various ways. They may project ideas of some projects which are worthy enough to promote, into the minds of (some) students who are in physical embodiment. Many Ascended Masters establish and maintain a focus of Their own in an Etheric

City. This gives Them a sort of step-down or in-between action and connection from the high vibratory action of Their Ascended Masters' Realm.

Around the Etheric Cities is a force, a belt or sphere which nothing of a slower vibration can penetrate; as there is also around each planet.

The **Teton Retreat** is also referred to as the Royal Teton and the Rocky Mountain Retreat. It is the first created Retreat on Earth. It was in this vicinity where the first Manu and people of the first root race came forth, and then expanded all over the Earth.

This Retreat is a physical Focus located in the Grand Teton Mountain, in the Teton Range in Wyoming, about two thousand feet from the top. The audience hall or Sanctuary is around one hundred feet wide, two hundred feet long (from north to south) and about fifty feet high with arched ceiling. A golden disc about twelve feet in diameter is in the center of the ceiling, within which is a seven-pointed star of yellow diamonds. The Secret Love Star pours through this. There are two circles of light around the disc, each about twelve inches in width, one a deep rose and the outer one of violet color. (These may vary at times.) Seven discs representing the seven rays and the seven planets are around the central disc; each with a diameter of about two feet, through which the Seven Elohim pour Their rays. The rest of the ceiling is sky blue. These discs are used by the Cosmic Beings at times as a focus to pour Their great currents of energy through to the Ascended Masters, Who direct it out over the

Earth, through nature and to the blessing of mankind. The ganglionic centers of both man and animal are directly affected by this radiation.

This Retreat is used as a focus for the outpouring from the Secret Love Star, the Seven Elohim and the Twelve Cosmic Beings, as well.

Portions of the walls are composed of white onyx, blue and rose granite and pure gold. This is of the natural formation as the Retreat was hewn out of the mountain.

There is an All-seeing Eye, about two feet in diameter in the wall at the north end of the room. It is about thirty-five feet from the floor. This is used to pour light rays through for specific purposes. This is the only place on Earth where there is a focus of this action. The Cosmic Mirror is in the east wall, towards the north end, about five feet from the floor. It is composed of a certain precipitated material; it is about thirty feet high and seventy feet long with a concave surface. It looks more like a mineral substance than a fabric, velvety in texture, and of a deep violet blue color. A Cosmic Mirror is used by the Great Ones for instructive purposes. They project upon it pictures from etheric records of lifestreams, the Earth and other planets, the past and present and it can also portray future events and activities.

There are a number of other rooms in which gold, jewels, treasures and records are kept. Here are the most complete records of Earth; there is a record of every civilization that has been on Earth. These records are physical and made by hand; the parts of them that were not available in the physical were made from the etheric records and therefore are accurate.

The Three-fold Flame stands in one room. There are a number of council chambers and other rooms, in which are musical instruments, art and music, inventions and formulas, all prepared and ready to be given to mankind for use in the new age.

Universal power is used for heat, light, power and cleansing purposes in the Retreats. When They produce a room by cutting out a portion of the mountain, They do it by the use of light rays and flame and there is no refuse left. The polishing is done by this same means.

There have been hewn out and added, seven rooms, representing the seven rays, around the audience hall, adjoining it like petals of a flower, which can be opened so the Altar is visible to all therein. The circular altar is in the center of the hall and is composed of Chinese ivory. At its base, in embossed gold, are plaques, depicting the evolutionary steps of the Earth.

These additional rooms were made necessary because of the great numbers of mankind attending in their inner bodies while asleep, as well as elementals and angels. The number attending has been increasing tremendously. All the disembodied, those who had been earth-bound, those from the sleepers' realm and so-called compound, have been drawn there at intervals. To provide for all these They created an amphitheater over the Retreat in the atmosphere, in the etheric realm.

Over the Teton Retreat in the etheric realm remains

the seven-fold lotus which was formed as the seven rays from the Seven Elohim were focused there through the bodies of the Seven Archangels when mankind first came to Earth. There was created the first Sanctuary.

It is at this Retreat where the Karmic Board convenes twice yearly (around the first of January and July). The Lords of Karma are seated in the atmosphere, in a semi-circle above the Altar in the Retreat, where the Lord of the World with Lord Maitreya and the Sponsor or Sponsors (the presiding Masters), of the year officiate.

Here each New Year's Eve at the close of the old year is received by the Lord of the World from the Planetary Silent Watcher the thought-form of the year, with its musical vibrations. This is the pattern (for the year) in which is the message or idea for each member of the Brotherhood to work out according to his perception and talents. The Lords of Karma then hear the petitions.

The service of the Brotherhood of the Teton Retreat (sometimes referred to as the Brotherhood of Precipitation), is to assist students to get back to having a conscious connection with their Source and Divinity. They help to open the proper channels for them (students) to receive the directions, activities and powers of light by which to attain mastery, the complete control of all energy which flows through them, and again have the enthusiasm they had in the beginning. They teach the purpose, plan and design of one's own life; one's reason for being; to become selfless which is complete surrender of self; return all to the Source; and have reverence of life.

Their service includes also the returning of the Earth to its original plan, purity and perfection. Their action is gratitude for life, radiation and expansion of the light. It is the Focus of precipitation and manifestation in the outer world. The Brotherhood encourage the development in their students of the understanding of the scientific method of precipitation.

The color of the **Precipitation Flame** is gold center with Chinese green edge.

The vicinity of the Teton is the place where the first root race came forth and then went forth from there, therefore this Focus represents the action of "going forth" —the precipitating of radiations, ideas, qualities, powers, and talents into the consciousnesses of unascended beings for the fulfillment of the divine plan. Missionaries go out from here.

The Brotherhood of the Teton usually wear white robes trimmed in green. The Ascended Master Lanto has been in charge of this Focus for a long time. He is ready to go on into greater service but instead He is accepting the Chohanship of the Second Ray, and the Ascended Master Confucius takes His place.

The Flame-flower may be the form of a calla lily or tulip, usually gold with green stem and leaves. (The Flame-flowers of the Retreats may vary in design from time to time, depending on the action at the Retreat.)

The keynote is "O, Thou Sublime Sweet Evening Star" from Tannhauser.

Shamballa on Earth was originally built by volunteers

from Venus who came some nine hundred years before Lord Sanat Kumara, to prepare a place for Him; thus the building of Shamballa began. These volunteers took one embodiment after another through that period of time.

It has been said that one hundred came at that time, and that three Kumaras and thirty others came with Him. He came to hold the light for the Earth, to sustain her and keep her place in the solar system.

Shamballa was built similar to or as a replica of the City of the Kumaras on the planet Venus, which is also called Shamballa and is the principal city there. The City of White was built upon the White Island, a precipitated island, in the Gobi Sea, which is now desert. A beautiful carved marble bridge connected the White Island with the mainland over a sapphire sea.

The central or main Temple with golden dome is somewhat elevated, with steps and terraces leading up to it. There is a Temple for each of the seven rays with its particular color. The Temples are mostly white with domes and spires. They stand along a beautiful wide avenue, lined with trees and bordered with flowers. There are terraces, beautiful flame-fountains and a pool with the blue birds of happiness (the mystic blue bird).

The main Temple is the Temple of the Lord of the World. It is all white, several hundred feet long, with an arched ceiling. Sanat Kumara's Star is suspended from the ceiling over the altar, which is more than twenty feet high. Marble steps lead up to it in several tiers. The Three-fold Flame was established here when Lord Sanat

Kumara came. It is the cohesive action for the Earth, and a thread of light from It connects with the Flame in the heart of every individual. It is this action that has sustained each one through the centuries.

Upon entering the main Temple, in a vase by the door, appears the favorite flowers of each one as he enters. He then is given an elixir to drink which gives him renewed or increased strength.

Shamballa was built three times in the physical and destroyed by cataclysmic action. Some memory of its physical existence over sixty thousand years ago, is recorded in occult literature. The Shamballa known to us now is in the etheric realm over the Gobi Desert.

When Lord Sanat Kumara came the Karmic Board gave much of the authority to Him for the working out of the salvation of Earth. He began by forming the Great White Brotherhood; Divine Beings volunteered Their services. He then magnetized through divine love, unascended beings to be trained to qualify for these positions in the future.

Individuals were drawn there through Sanat Kumara's love and trained as messengers who then went forth carrying the message of love and the reason for His coming. When individuals understood sufficiently and qualified, they were made members of the Great White Brotherhood.

They return to Shamballa once each year and offer their harvest to the Lord of the World. They have a period of rest, that is sort of a vacation time, when they may come back into the radiation there, and that of the Lord of the World; after which they get their new assignments for the coming year.

The three kingdoms bring their harvest which is the essence of energy used in the year's endeavors of impersonal service. The Angelic Host are the first to bring Their harvest. They have Their ceremony on Michael's Day, September twenty-ninth. The elementals have their ceremony the latter part of October, Halloween time. The Great White Brotherhood and students (in their inner bodies), have their harvest ceremony the latter part of November. In the outer world we have our Thanksgiving Day as an expression of gratitude.

Shamballa was opened for the first time November 15, 1952, to mankind.

Sanat Kumara was given His Freedom in January nineteen fifty-six; after ceremonies at Shamballa He attended ceremonies at the Temple of Faith over the locality of Banff and from there returned to Venus for the first time upon receiving His Freedom from exile on Earth for these millions of years. The banner of Lord Gautama now flies over Shamballa in place of Lord Sanat Kumara's banner (a purple background with a laurel wreath around the planet Venus, upon it), which has been there since His coming to Earth. Lord Gautama's banner has a golden background with the design of the spheres of the seven rays surrounding the Earth, upon it.

The color of the Flame at this Focus is pink, gold and blue. The keynote is now "Song of India" since Lord

Gautama's ascent; formerly it was "Caprice Viennois."

The **Retreat at Ceylon**—Temple of Comfort—is on the Island of Ceylon off the coast of Southern India. It is underneath a tea plantation. The building above ground is situated on a promontory, but underneath is a marvelous Retreat. The Flame room is below this building. It is done in pink, trimmed in gold, the walls are pink with pink carpet on the floor; the chairs, too, are pink. There are pictures of the Seven Chohans on the walls. The magnificent chalice on the Altar, holding the **Comfort Flame** has small carved white ivory doves (clustered) around the edge. The Comfort Flame is white in the center, but mostly pink radiance with some gold.

This Retreat is the Lord Maha Chohan's Focus on Earth, through which He pours His energy and blessings to nature. He pours His blessings through the Flame room to the nature kingdom. He is the magnet for the energies used on Earth. He magnetizes that energy from the Sun in great streams or currents of energy and as it comes into the atmosphere of Earth it is diffused into the seven colors of the rays: before that it is pure white light. These are then diverted to the Seven Chohans. They magnetize the rays; Each then tempers His ray as required, diffuses and directs it into the kingdoms of man, elemental and Angel. The Angels absorb and intensify it, the elementals also have a tendency to intensify it, but man absorbs instead of intensifying it and radiating it out.

This Retreat is dedicated to education, and is the Focus of training for those who desire to become a comfort to life, or endeavor to become future Maha Chohans or who are to become representatives of the Holy Spirit. The action of the Retreat represents the completeness of spiritual endeavors in this realm. It is also headquarters for the Seven Chohans for Their general councils, since They are under the direction of the Lord Maha Chohan.

All channels and activities in the outer world which pertain to the well-being of mankind and the comfort of all life come under this Retreat and the supervision of the Lord Maha Chohan.

The predominant qualities of the Retreat are love, grace, humility and selflessness. It was opened for the first time May 15, 1952, to mankind. The Lord Maha Chohan is in charge of this Retreat. Djwal Kul is Sponsor and welcomes the guests during the time it is open. The banner of the Lord Maha Chohan has a white dove, representative of Himself, from which pour forth seven rays, upon a purple field representing the activity of the Freedom Flame. The dove symbolizes the animation of the Freedom Flame and the Seventh Ray.

The Flame is similar to a white water lily or lotus with pink edges. The keynote is "At Dawning," by Cadman.

The **Retreat at Darjeeling**—Temple of the Will of God—is located on the outskirts of Darjeeling in the foothills of the Himalayan Mountains in India.

This Focus has been there for a thousand years, but the architecture of the buildings is of a later date. It is surrounded by English gardens, and marble steps lead up to the large entrance doors which are gold. A replica of the

Taj Mahal is in the central hall and tapestries depicting scenes of King Arthur's Court are on the wall. A beautiful drawing room is to the left of the hall with a fireplace, grand piano, desk and other furnishings. The council chamber is on the right side of the entrance hall. There is a stairway on both sides of the entrance hall. There is a tower with a dome at each end, a story higher than the main building. One of these is made into an astronomical observatory, a Sanctuary in the other tower. The Sanctuary is done in white and royal blue; a blue carpet is on the floor. The Altar is crystal with sapphire and diamonds; on it is a golden chalice holding a replica of the Earth which contains the original pattern for this planet.

This is the Focus in which the Will of God is represented, and is the action of the magnetizing of divine ideas.

The Brothers of the Diamond Heart, in Their activities and services to life, is the guarding and protecting of spiritual foci which have been created as heart centers of religious or political world movements. The Brotherhood wear white garments with the emblem, a diamond heart over the heart, and a blue cape.

The Ascended Master Morya is in charge of this Retreat. When officiating He usually wears a white robe and turban banded in royal blue and heavily decorated with diamonds and sapphires.

This Restreat was opened to mankind April 15, 1953, for the first time.

The Flame is white with blue radiance, and may take

the form of a diamond heart. The keynote of the Retreat is "Pomp and Circumstance" by Elgar.

During the Theosophical days He had His Home, a Focus at Shigatse, Tibet.

The **Focus of Wisdom**—Temple of Wisdom, is in the ethers over the hills of Kashmir, India. It is also called the Cathedral of Nature. There is no building, just a Focus in the etheric realm with the natural beauty of nature surrounding it.

Its activity is to give assistance to lifestreams on Earth to again have the activity of the Christ Self function through the outer self.

This is a Focus of the Brothers of the Golden Robe, and an action of the Second Ray. The Brothers of the Golden Robe are the Teachers of mankind, through illumined obedience and inspiration; They formulate ideas into a workable plan, pattern and design. The Brothers of the Golden Robe also have Temples in the Second Sphere where instruction on the law is given to those who are in between embodiments. Particularly those who are to take embodiment again are instructed here, also those in embodiment while they sleep, go there for instruction in their finer bodies.

This Focus was opened for the first time March 15, 1953, with the outpouring of Lord Maitreya (through Jesus for the Easter Season).

The Ascended Master Kuthumi is in charge of this Focus. The Flame-flower is a yellow-gold lotus. The keynote is "Kashmiri Song (Pale Hands I Love.)"

Kuthumi has a Home, a Focus in the physical at Shigatse, Tibet. There are caves extending for miles, and in them is a semi-tropical temperature. Therein is a replica of every change of Earth's surface, and many other records and treasures.

The **Chateau de Liberté**—Temple of Liberty, is on the Rhone River in Southern France. There is a most beautiful garden surrounding it with a pool and marble fountains, and an abundance of roses; around the columns of the building are climbing roses; marble steps lead up to the entrance. The wide entrance doors have encrusted on the white panel of each a dove in gold. The entrance hall has a marble floor with a mosaic pattern over the focus of the Liberty Flame in the room or Sanctuary below. When standing on this spot the pulsations of the **Liberty Flame** can be felt. From the entrance hall there is a marble stairway on either side leading down to the floor below into a hall from which extends the corridor to the audience hall or Flame room. This beautiful long mirrored hall is a likeness of the Hall of Mirrors at Versailles. There are paintings of the Archangels by Paul, the Venetian Master, between these mirrors.

The audience hall seats less than one hundred persons. It is a small Retreat compared to some. The Altar is crystal and on it is a hand which holds the golden chalice with the Liberty Flame in it. This Flame is pink, gold and blue, the perfect balance of love, wisdom and power. A picture of the Lord Maha Chohan is above the Altar with the symbol of the dove over His heart. There are pictures of the Seven Chohans on the walls. The chairs are of French design and arranged in groups of seven.

The Liberty Flame is three-fold, the perfect balance of love, wisdom and power; pink, gold and blue. It was brought to Earth by the Goddess of Liberty in the beginning and established in the Temple of the Sun where New York City is now. There was a central Temple with twelve around it. These still stand in the etheric realm over that locality. Chelas admitted to those Temples learn how to expand that Flame and express beauty and perfection. The Three-fold Flame within the heart gives one liberty to use life, to magnetize, qualify and radiate light. Its design is liberty and Its destiny is full mastery.

Some of the Liberty Flame in the Temple of Liberty located in the vicinity of New York City on Atlantis, was taken to France before the sinking of Poseidonis. It has been preserved in this Retreat through the centuries. It was this Liberty Flame that inspired many a patriot of the American Revolutionary War and It was a cause back of the assistance that came to America from France. It was through the radiation of this Flame (and of course the Ascended Master Saint Germain's efforts), that prompted and sustained the enthusiasm of the French to give that great and unprecedented assistance to America during the Revolutionary War. It was their efforts which brought about America's freedom. Later an action of that Flame was returned to New York through the Statue of Liberty. Everyone that enters the harbor, when going by the Statue of Liberty, their heart feels that flame and most people also are aware of it in their feelings. It may be like a strange feeling they do not understand.

The action of this Retreat is to liberate and develop their own individual talents and powers, and express beauty. Herein is a beautiful collection of the various arts. Many rare paintings and sculptures; outstanding writings from ancient civilizations as well as more recent ones, are possessions of this Retreat.

This is a Focus of the Third Ray. The service of the Brotherhood of Liberty is giving assistance to development and cultivation of the Three-fold Flame and of natural talents.

This Retreat was first opened to mankind September 15, 1953. The Ascended Paul, the Venetian Master, is in charge. The Flame is the Three-fold Flame, pink, gold and blue. The keynote is "The Marseillaise."

The **Retreat at Luxor**—Ascension Temple, is near the Nile River in the desert of Egypt. There is a large square white building made of stone with a high wall surrounding it. There is a large and beautiful courtyard with fountains and nearly every species of flower and bird, for the purpose of the perpetuation of them.

The Ascension Flame was taken by Serapis to that locality just before the sinking of Poseidonis. He established It there and in later embodiments built a Temple around It. The present subterranean Retreat was built during the decline of Egypt, one building has been retained above ground. The entrance to the Ascension Temple is through this white building. There are other buildings below the earth's surface which are used by the Brother-hood of Luxor.

The **Ascension Temple** is built in a square; in construc-tion, it is composed of tall columns, twelve on each side; these are whitish or colorless. The Temples, one within the other, are the action of the seven rays. The first room or square is blue representing the first ray. The next is a square within that, which is yellow, then within that is the pink and so on for the seven rays, each one formed by large columns. The Flame room which composes the center is all white. There are no doors between the col-umns, the dividing line being formed by radiation of the respective rays. The outer Temple is large and can ac-commodate a great number of people. A neophyte coming into the Retreat knows only the outermost room. It being the activity of the blue, he would not see beyond that or into the next one, he would have no idea there was an-other room, another portion of the building there, until his consciousness was raised and he was prepared to enter the vibratory action of the next section whereupon he would simply walk in, between some pillars.

The Altar is in the center of the Flame room and is shaped like a pyramid, on the top of which is an Egyptian urn holding the **Ascension Flame.** The chelas encircle the Altar, at ceremonies. The activity of twelve is used throughout this Retreat. The twelve virtues of the God-head (which the zodiacal signs represent) are represented around the Altar.

There is a collection of valuable fine arts, and a great

library of rare books accessible to those admitted to the Retreat, with no instruction as to what pursuit to follow.

Absolute obedience is a demand of the Brotherhood of the Ascension at Luxor, in Their Retreat, where the demand for complete obedience is inflexible. They give training in controlling vibration and energy, and the mastery of substance.

The Ascension Flame gives assistance to those who have turned from desires of the outer and make effort to the attainment of the Ascension and fulfill their destiny. The Brotherhood have sustained the Ascension Flame since It was taken there. The discipline is strict and therefore it is not an inducement for students to go there. This Brotherhood has always been small in numbers because of the severity of discipline required in this Retreat.

This Focus is the activity of the Fourth Ray, and with the assistance of the Brotherhood the dormant, deep rooted qualities and the last vestige of one's human creation is brought forth to be transmuted. When it is done, this enables the Ascension to take place.

The Ascension Flame raises the vibratory action of an individual; at a certain point of frequency It neutralizes or cuts the gravity pull and serves as a bridge from the human existence into the Divine—the Ascended State. The Ascension Flame gives one the feeling of new life, hope and buoyancy. It is the sustaining power of enthusiasm. This Ascension Flame contains within It the momentum of all Ascensions from the Earth since It was established.

Every lifestream taking embodiment for whom it is possible to attain the Ascension is sponsored by One from the Brotherhood of the Ascension. The Ascension Flame is essential to every lifestream to the attainment of the Ascension, which is the completion of each one's journeying on Earth.

Many thousands of individuals have the opportunity now to be prepared to make the Ascension at inner levels without having to re-embody. These lifestreams are taken to the Ascension Temples in the inner realms and there they are taught the Law and given assistance of the Ascension Flame. The dispensation for this was obtained January 1, 1954, by Archangel Michael. The Ascension Temples at inner levels were opened April 14, 1954, to all those who came under the dispensation, whereby they would not have to re-embody but could make the Ascension from there. These Temples with about forty-foot doors, are all white and have the capacity to seat thousands of persons.

The Retreat at Luxor represents the action of drawing-in, or completing the cycle of Earth's evolution; while the Teton Retreat represents the going forth.

The Brotherhood usually wear white robes with crystal trimmings at the hem and cuffs and a sun over the heart. The headdress has a golden band with a sun and with wings of flame on either side, on the forehead.

The motto of the Retreat is "Try."

This Retreat was opened September 15, 1952 to mankind for the first time.

The Ascended Master Serapis Bey is in charge of this Retreat.

The Flame is white or crystal. The Flame-flower is similar to the Easter lily. The keynote is "Liebestraum" by Franz Liszt.

The **Temple of Truth,** this Focus is at present in the etheric realm, in the atmosphere above the ruins of the physical building. This building had been built during the centuries after the sinking of Atlantis, on what is now known as the Island of Crete; it was then a part of the mainland of what is now Greece. A portion of the Flame had been carried from the Temple on Atlantis in one of the boats to that location. The building at Crete was very similar in structure to the Temple on Atlantis, with the large, tall columns, and similar to the Parthenon. Destructive individuals destroyed the physical building as the true Grecian culture declined. The etheric Temple is a replica of the former, but is very large. It has beautiful marble steps (around four hundred) , leading up to the entrance door which is between huge columns. The frieze all around the building is of gold.

The Altar is around one hundred feet in height, with a large pillar, beautifully carved, on either side. The **Flame of Truth** is contained in golden braziers upon them. The Altar is entwined with green ivy; They usually use the ivy and calla lily-like flame-flowers for decorative purposes.

The positions of the Brothers and Sisters of Truth are designated by mosaic patterns in the marble floor.

The Brotherhood of Truth render service to the people

who have a "vocation," and They reveal truth concerning it (their particular vocation) , no matter on what ray they are.

The Cosmic Being Vesta was the first Goddess of Truth for the Earth. Ascended Lady Master Pallas Athena took that position a long time ago. She is the embodiment of that virtue.

After the building was destroyed there were the Delphic Oracles through whom the Truth was conveyed to seekers of Truth. The Oracles of the Delphi Order received their truths from beloved Ascended Beings Vesta and Pallas Athena. This lasted for about seven hundred years before impurity entered in, through one individual, which resulted in the disconnection of the contacts with the Ascended Ones. Those recorded truths are still held in the Retreat. Pallas Athena, the Goddess of Truth, Who represents Cosmic Truth to the Earth is patroness of this Focus. She was known to mankind in earlier ages and had a direct connection with seekers of Truth through the Delphic Oracles, until there was such perversion that She had to withdraw.

The Brotherhood of Truth abide herein, directing the Flame of Truth into the consciousness of mankind for their understanding and acceptance which enables them to comprehend the eternal Truths. The Brotherhood give assistance to agnostics, the disillusioned, sceptics and doubters. Here the disillusioned regain faith, courage and strength. Hilarion and the Brotherhood of Truth direct from here the Flame of Truth to those calling for truth.

They enfold all messengers and missionaries going forth to present what they believe to be truth. Religious teachers, Messiahs and Avatars are all members of this Brotherhood. Sincere seekers of Truth go to the Temple in their inner bodies while asleep.

The symbol of the Brotherhood is a lamp or brazier from which emits the Flame of Truth, They have this emblem on their garments over the heart. The garments of the Brotherhood are white with bands of green on the sleeves and at the hem. Sometimes when officiating in ceremonies They wear robes of green.

This Focus was opened to mankind October 15, 1953 for the first time.

The Ascended Master Hilarion is the Chohan in charge of this Focus. This is the Focus of the Fifth Ray for the Earth.

The Flame of Truth is green with a white center. The white Flame taking the form similar to the calla lily (or tulip) forming the Flame-flower with bright or Chinese green radiance. "Onward Christian Soldiers" (a hymn) holds within it the melody of the keynote of this Focus.

The **Arabian Retreat** is northeast of the Red Sea beneath the sands of Arabia. The buildings are of a former civilization which were sunk in cataclysmic activity, hermetically sealed by Ascended Masters, and later the sands completely covered them. They are more than a hundred feet below the surface, with good ventilation.

The audience hall contains a design of the zodiac in the floor in the center. Here various inventions have been perfected and then given to some one in the outer world for their production. The television room is specially insulated and contains a "reflector"; through this instrument can be seen any event or place at any point on Earth, simply by turning a dial. It has been used in the Retreat for over a hundred years. There is a radio room, and a radio which can pick up sound anywhere on Earth. The Cosmic Ray room is where the use of light rays is taught; in the art room new arts and colors are produced; in another room are musical instruments and compositions which will be used in the new age; and another room where some of the Brothers are trained for governmental positions. There is also a place where many records and great riches are kept.

It was said that before Jesus' time Lord Tabor was in charge of this Retreat, and then the Ascended Master Jesus took charge of It.

This Retreat in Arabia (in the near East) was opened March 15, 1952, for the first time to the consciousness of mankind. It was the first one to open in this new action of opening the various Retreats one at a time for a period of a month. Here are the Brothers of the Indigo Cape.

The **Retreat at Transylvania**—Temple of Freedom, is located in the foothills of the Carpathian Mountains in Transylvania, Hungary. Here is a mansion in the natural beauty of the mountains; a path leading up to the entrance. The door is beautifully carved. This Retreat is rather small and the grounds are not large.

Seating capacity in the Flame room is around a hundred persons. Upon the Altar is the **Freedom Flame,** an action of the Three-fold Flame, the **Violet Flame** being the radiance, an action of It.

The three-fold action of the Violet Flame is, the main portion violet, with pink center and outer radiance blue.

The Freedom Flame was safely transported by Saint Germain to a place of safety and security in Europe (Transylvania), before Archangel Zadkiel's physical Temple was removed from what is now Cuba.

Here in Transylvania through the past centuries research has gone on by alchemists, particularly for an elixir to prolong life. Many well known persons in history were guests here in the Focus of Freedom, where they received inspiration, wisdom and assistance to further their cause for good. Here is a collection of rare treasures of things. that belonged to some patriot or someone who played a part in great historical events. The Ascended Master Saint Germain has already moved much from His Retreat in Transylvania to His Retreat in the Rockies in the United States.

There was constructed May 15, 1954, in the etheric realm a Temple of the Violet Flame in the form of a Maltese cross over this Retreat, to be a permanent Focus in the lower atmosphere.

This Retreat was opened for the first time to mankind July 15, 1952.

The Ascended Master Saint Germain is in charge. The Flame is violet or purple; purple violets being the Flame-flower. The keynote is in the Waltzes by Johann Strauss.

To cut oneself free from destructive forces and connections of this embodiment and all former ones the following application can be used. First give attention and love to the I AM Presence and feel the Christ Self (Higher Mental Body) envelop your hand and arm, visualizing a sword of blue flame in your hand. Then with your physical hand go through the motion of cutting down all around you with the sword, turning your body around until the circle is completed; severing all ties and strings connecting you with forces outside of yourself which may be anywhere on Earth or in its atmosphere. Then ask the Presence and Christ Self to blaze forth light rays to the furthest ends of the lines of force connected with you and transmute them all the way back to you. That way one can get rid of a lot of imperfect karma in a short time. One can also call to the I AM Presence, Cosmic Being Astrea and Archangel Michael to lock the Cosmic Circle and Sword of Blue Flame around himself and transmute whatever is not of the light.

The **Resurrection Temple** is in the etheric realm and is not of physical structure. The Temple is white and circular in form. It has around it seven circular corridors of various or graded degrees of radiation. The **Resurrection Flame** is in the central part of the Temple and opalescent in color.

Krishna seeing the need, first drew the Resurrection Flame into the atmosphere of Earth after mankind had begun to generate the various qualities of imperfection. He established It in the etheric realm over what is now known as the Holy Land.

The action and power of this Flame is resurrection, resuscitation and restoration by increasing the vibratory action of the electrons in the cells. It is uplifting, life-giving and produces hope and buoyancy. An action of the Resurrection Flame is, It will reverse the currents of energy. It turns imperfection into perfection or produces out of it perfection. It is the hope for all mankind.

This Flame enables individuals to maintain life in the body for long periods of time. The Spirit of Resurrection will resuscitate for man his faculties and resurrect his body into perfection and mastery when given opportunity. It does it in nature and brings forth from the dormant state the green vegetation and flowers in the Springtime. It is by use of the Resurrection Flame that Spring is made manifest.

The Lord Maha Chohan works much from this Temple. This is the Focus of the Directors of the Elements and the Forces of Nature.

The Resurrection Flame was made physically manifest through Jesus after the crucifixion; through It His physical body was etherealized in the tomb. That was the example of Its power to be left for mankind. This is the reason the crucifixion was permitted to take place. The Ascended Masters Jesus and Mary are in charge of this Focus. They assumed this responsibility of the Resurrection Flame after Their Ascension, because They worked with and used It so much in Their final lifetimes on Earth.

The Brothers and Sisters of the Resurrection wear white robes with opalescent bands on the sleeves and at the hem.

This Temple was opened May 15, 1953 to mankind, for the first time.

The Resurrection Flame is predominantly white with rainbow colors as of mother of pearl through it. The lily is the symbol of Resurrection. The keynote for the Focus is "A Perfect Day"; Ave Maria can also be used to draw the radiation.

The **Retreat of the Blue Lotus** is in one of the high mountain peaks of the Himalayan Mountains in Tibet. It is in one of several mountain peaks, which is designated to the chela by the outline of the Master's head on the bare rock at the entrance place. It is said that a large profile of a face can be seen on the side of that mountain in which is Lord Himalaya's Retreat, by students, neophytes, or chelas seeking entrance; it is perhaps not seen by others, but that guidance enables them to find it.

The top of that mountain is cone shaped. Within it are seven chambers hewn out of the mountain, in tier fashion. The entrance is somewhat down on the mountain side and enters into the lowest chamber. At the entrance is a pool which contains blue lotus flowers.

The seating is oriental fashion arranged on wide marble steps going up from the back to the front where the Altar is, in a gradual incline. As a neophyte enters the Retreat he knows of only this one chamber; as he advances he is admitted to the next one above and so on to the seventh. There is a door behind the Altar which can be slid wide open, thus connecting with the next five chambers, thereby having the seven chambers all open at once and appear as one (continuous) large amphitheater at the top of which can be seen the **Blue Lotus Flame** on the Altar, from the lowest step. The Flame is in a fount of purple jade and rises in blue lotus flames. Behind this stands a huge statue of Lord Gautama in gold.

Some records and treasures have been transferred from this Retreat to Lord Meru's Retreat in South America.

The action and qualities of this Focus are enlightenment, illumination, peace and tranquility. The first impulse went forth from here April 15, 1952 when this new action was set up. It was opened to mankind in general on March 15, 1954, with an official ceremony on March twentieth. Of course that means they (mankind) were permitted to go there in their finer (inner) bodies, most of them while asleep. Those who were not invited inside received the blessings of the radiation there.

This is a very sacred Focus of Light because one of the Permanent Rays (the masculine aspect) is focused through it.

Lord Himalaya, Manu of the fourth root race is in charge of this Focus.

The Brotherhood wear yellow robes. The Flame-flower is a blue lotus. The Keynote is "Love's Old Sweet Song."

The **Retreat—Temple of Illumination,** is an ancient

Focus. It is also known as the "Mount of Attainment." It is located in Mount Meru near Lake Titicaca in the Andes Mountains in South America. It is hewn right out of the mountain. This is where the Permanent Ray of the feminine aspect enters the Earth and is therefore considered very sacred. The masculine Ray has been active through the ages, now the feminine one becomes active. Through these Foci flow the currents of spiritual impetus to/for the people embodying on Earth. This (feminine) ray is the fertility or manifest expression of the God ideas for the Earth.

The entrance to the Retreat is through a lodge where people, mountain climbers, may stop over and rest. There is no indication of a Retreat being there from the outer standpoint.

The entrance door is behind a curtain at the end of the lodge, which one enters only by invitation. This door opens into a long hallway which leads to the Temple of Illumination. This Flame room is a cave in the mountain. The **Flame of Illumination** abides in a natural cave. Individual pink and gold cushions on the floor is the seating arrangement; these are placed in a semi-circle around the Flame. The seating capacity is around three hundred persons. However, they have recently added two wings to this, one on each side, wherein have been placed chairs. Their activities are carried on in an informal manner. There is no Altar, the Flame is just there in a pillar of light.

Certain records have been transferred from Retreats

in the East to this Retreat for future use as the new age progresses.

This is a Focus of the Second Ray, the action of education. The Brothers of the Golden Robe work through this Focus. The Brothers of Illumination wear robes of yellow-gold trimmed with pink roses at the hem and cuffs and a pink rose over the heart. The Brotherhood of this Retreat is small in numbers.

The pink rose is the symbol of this Retreat. It was opened to mankind August 15, 1952 for the first time. Lord Meru and Goddess Meru are in charge of this Focus. The Flame is yellow-gold with pink radiance, the very center being white. The keynote is "Faith of Our Fathers."

The **Retreat of Lord Tabor** is in the American Rocky Mountains; an extremely beautiful place, produced by the glories of nature. It is vastly jeweled by her, crystal being used abundantly; there is a fountain of rainbow hues. It is illumined through a radiant action of constantly changing colors. Lord Tabor governs the power of the Rocky Mountain Range from this Focus.

The **Cave of Symbols** is the Ascended Master Saint Germain's Retreat in America. It is in the Rocky Mountains in or near Wyoming. It has been there for hundreds of centuries.

There is a medium sized cavern at the entrance, from the ceiling of which hang various colored stalactites of many occult symbols. At the far end of the cavern are three arches (of various colors for different occasions). These open into a domed, twelve-angled room of various colors. It is about sixty feet in diameter. Here is the radio of three planes of operation, invented by Leonora, with a transparent case. Next to this room is the chemical laboratory; then comes the electrical laboratory. Here is the Atomic Accelerator, a chair of golden color, without mechanism; the instrument which increases the vibratory action of the atoms of the body and raises it, even into the Ascension.

About one hundred feet underneath is a large room wherein are produced the materials and devices used in the laboratories, everything operated by a form of electricity.

There is a reception room, at the level of the laboratories, which opens into sleeping quarters and the audience hall. The hall is about forty by eighty feet, with domed sky-colored ceiling and radiant walls. There is a piano and an organ in it and whatever is required for the occasion for which the hall is being used. Saint Germain uses it for a banquet room as well as an audience hall. The Cosmic Mirror (twelve by twenty feet) is on the east wall.

The room called the Sphere of Light is entered through a concealed door in the wall at the far end of the audience hall. The shape of it is a sphere. It is used to intensify the expansion of the light in individuals.

The **Secret Valley** is in the mountains in the region of Tucson, Arizona. It is entered through a tunnel which is concealed to the outer world. It consists of a space of around one hundred acres, is very beautiful, semi-tropical, with an abundance of various fruits, vegetables and nuts. There is a lovely waterfall at one end of the valley, near the ancient building, which is magnificent with its white onyx and pink marble interior. This is the Retreat of the Ascended Master Eriel.

The **Temple of Faith** and **Protection** is situated in the etheric realm over the vicinity of Banff and Lake Louise in the Canadian Rockies, extending over the border of the United States. It is composed of gold, diamonds and sapphires, and is tremendous in size. It has an entrance on each of the four sides, forty-nine steps leading up to the forty-foot doors of gold, inlaid in blue sapphires, a golden dome, and around the Temple are beautiful gardens with fountains and marble benches.

It was originally created out of the mountain (circular in shape), after the first root race came to Earth, for Archangel Michael's use. People from all over the world came to It to strengthen their faith in whatever project they were pursuing. It was used all through the ages before the destructive forces were generated. It was a physical manifestation then, this was later destroyed but the etheric Temple remained. This has been closed to the outer mind and mankind in general since then, but it was opened for the first time on January 15, 1956, to the students in the outer world that they may go there in their inner bodies while asleep, during the time It is open.

The Altar containing the **Flame of Faith** (white and blue) is in the center and it is composed of diamonds. The seats circle around it.

Elementals, angels and men come here to renew their faith, strength, courage and to be re-charged with enthusiasm which enables them to go on rendering the service they have undertaken.

Archangel Michael is in charge of this Focus from which He and His Legions have served mankind throughout the ages.

The keynote of this Focus is "Soldiers' Chorus" from Faust.

The **Temple of Purification** was physically manifest on Atlantis where Cuba is now, up to the time of the sinking of the continent. It was known all over the world then. The priests and priestesses transported their bodies by levitation and went wherever the requirement was. That way great assistance was enabled to be given anywhere on the Earth's surface.

There were seven Temples at various locations, but the main one in which Lord Zadkiel presided was in the center. The others were similar in action but smaller. These were a tremendous Focus of purification. They were dedicated to the transmutation of mis-qualified energies on Earth. Here was taught the use and power of conscious invocation.

They are all in the etheric realm over Cuba now. These Temples retained the training at inner levels of divine alchemy to initiates after Atlantis sank. The main Temple is similar to that of Lord Michael's. It is circular in shape and very large, with four entrances, and a golden dome.

It is made of gold with encrusted amethysts. The Altar on which is the Violet Flame is in the center.

It is presided over by Archangels Zadkiel and Amethyst. The Brotherhood are known as the Order of Zadkiel, which was established when the Temples were physical, and is a branch of the "White Order." The priests and priestesses of the Order, rendered services through the action called darsham (utilizing one's accumulated good). This Focus is an action of the Seventh Ray. It was opened October 15, 1957, to mankind. Keynote is Blue Danube Waltz.

The **Palace of Light**—Chananda's Home and the Cave of Light is in a beautiful valley in the Himalayan Mountains. It is about two miles wide and four miles in length from east to west with a stream running through it, and a waterfall at the west end; a high cliff on the north side, semi-tropical climate, and an abundance of fruits and vegetables. This valley has been there as it is today, for twenty centuries or more. No word or feeling of discord has entered the Home through the centuries. The outside entrance is sealed and appears as solid rock, so no one from the outer world will detect it.

There is a magnificent four story building of white onyx, with a large dome over the center. This is the Home of the Ascended Master Chananda and His Sister Najah, also Ascended.

They have an electrical laboratory as well as a chemical laboratory for the purpose of experimental work. A cosmic observatory is under the dome. Here is an instrument called the Absorption Reflector, and other instruments not known to scientists of the outer world. There is a light projector and television set (which they had long before television was known to mankind).

The audience hall covers nearly all of one floor of the building, and seats around seven hundred persons. It is in white onyx, trimmed in blue with blue carpet on the floor, and a Golden Altar at the side. There is a piano and organ like those in the Cave of Symbols.

The **Cave of Light** is behind the palace in the mountain. The entrance is through a concealed door in the west wall on the ground floor of the palace. The door opens into a passage about one half mile long, leading to the Cave, where there is a carved door opening into a large cave. Here are also stalactites similar to those in the Cave of Symbols. Doors of gold open into the Cave of Light. The light drawn into this cave is a consciously drawn focus of Cosmic Light, which appears as a white fire. This completely transmutes all human propensities for those who enter and they are freed from all limitations. Of course no one gains entrance except by invitation and direction of the Ascended Ones. This is the Cosmic Being Divine Director's Focus, and thousands have been set free through Its assistance.

The Divine Director began to draw the light and action from this Cave of Light into the class rooms in March nineteen thirty-eight, for the blessing of the students. Before that the students always had to go to the Retreats for such actions.

The **Temple of Mercy** is located over the foothills outside of Peiping (Peking), China, in the etheric realm. The main Temple or Pagoda with golden dome is on an elevation above the twelve others surrounding it, with inclined domes towards the main one. The doors of the Temple are hand carved. Silence has been maintained in it for centuries. The Altar is of carved ivory upon which is a lotus cup or urn containing the **Flame of Mercy.** Its action and qualities are mercy, forgiveness, transmutation, compassion and a tremendous feeling of peace.

Kwan Yin, the Goddess of Mercy, is in charge of this Focus.

The Temple of Mercy was opened for the first time February 15, 1953, to mankind.

The Brothers and Sisters of this Temple wear soft purple colored silk robes. The color of the Flame is purple. The keynote of the Retreat is "In a Monastery Garden."

The **Palace of White Marble** is deep in the heart of the mountains of India. This very beautiful Temple stands on the site of a basin towered by mountain peaks. The building faces east, is of white marble, has a central dome of gold, with a smaller one on each of the four corners. The interior also is white, with decorative touches of various colors; the material is imperishable. The Council Chamber is under the large dome; in it is a beautiful large jade table with veins of gold running through it. A semi-tropical climate is maintained there. This is a great Focus of Light, created by the Great White Brotherhood many centuries ago.

The **Retreat Northeast of Suva** is in an island in the Fiji Islands in the South Pacific. These islands were a part of the continent of Mu. The Retreat was in the high mountains before the sinking of the continent. This was the Focus of the Cosmic Being Surya when the fourth root race was beginning to come into embodiment. The third and fourth root races came in at this location.

The island is seldom seen and no ships land there because the Masters control that through the ocean currents. Today this Retreat is a magnificent city under the ocean, with one beautiful building on the surface. Hundreds of people have been rescued from drowning, never knowing how they were saved, and taken there. They were given time to adjust to the vibratory action and then given definite training; none ever rebelled against the discipline required in the Retreat.

The Ascended Master Cuzco is in charge of the Retreat. His Home has been there for one million, four hundred thousand years or more. It has been a mighty Focus of light for a very long time. They have held (in Their hands, so to speak) the control of the poles, and govern cataclysmic actions of Earth. They have inventions and things there, the simplicity of which is marvelous.

The particular quality is peace and tranquility; the action is that of extreme love and protection. Cuzco gave a dictation July 25, 1939, to the students. The Brotherhood of Suva opened the Retreat for the first time October 15, 1952, to mankind. The Keynote is "Aloha Oe".

The **Retreat on the Island of Madagascar,** near South

Africa, is a great Focus and one of the oldest in the world. The Goddess of Purity works from/through this Focus. No boats ever land there, because the waters swirl so that they can't; that is how They have it protected. It was said that the island has been above water a million years; as has also the peninsula of California.

The **Shrine of Glory**, the Goddess of Light's Focus is in the Andes Mountains in South America.

Elohim Hercules' Focus of Light is in Yosemite Park in California.

There is a Focus of Light of the Great White Brotherhood on Mount Shasta and Mount Whitney in the United States of America; in the jungles of Brazil, South America, is a City of great perfection.

The Brotherhood has a Focus in a residential section at Calcutta, India, in a magnificent building owned by Them, where Their Councils meet; and an ancient Temple also near the city, where some mighty work is going on in a subterranean room. They have another Focus at Benares, India, in a beautiful building, the interior is of pink and white marble, decorated with gold, with no lighting fixtures.

A Castle overlooking the city of Paris is the Focus of The Council of France. The Head of it is an Ascended Master, Who ascended more than five hundred years ago. He was Ascended Leto's father in a former embodiment and Her Teacher in Her last lifetime.

The Villa of the Ascended Masters K-17 and His Sister

is another Focus of Light and is in the vicinity of Paris.

The Cosmic Being Pelleur's Focus is in the center of the Earth, where there is the Sun of "Even Pressure" and continuous soft light; with vegetation of ivory and pink. This Focus, an action of the Three-fold Flame, radiates a pressure of the Silence and a balancing action. Complete harmony is maintained by the inhabitants.

It was once said that there were subterranean tunnels connecting the Grand Teton Retreat, the Cave of Symbols and Mount Whitney.

When addressing or calling to the Divine Beings, Their Names should be preceded with Their Divine Title, such as Ascended Master, Lord, God, Goddess, Cosmic Being, Cosmic Master, Archangel or Elohim. This will avoid tuning in and tying to other lifestreams who bear that same name.

In contemplation of the I AM Presence (the chart) there will come the full comprehension of what the Presence means to you.

Ask the Presence to give you the comprehension of these things, and show you through the feelings, the truth.

The quality that produces impatience is a lack of confidence. Patience is perfect control of the inner and outer energies. Patience is persistent application.

"The Middle Way" which holds a balance between the inner and outer activities, should be maintained.

Peace is a state of consciousness, when all of the four lower bodies are harmonious with each other and in accord with the I AM Presence, the God-Self, Peace is produced.

One must not let conditions deprive him of the harmony required to get his answers. Make the call two or three times a day and in between silently use the feeling to continue to repeat itself once an hour or twice an hour, so that that impulse goes forth.

The call for a thing releases a certain vibratory action which is needed by the student, for manifestation.

The decrees and songs in this activity have given us a way and means to accomplish cosmic actions.

The power of the Three times Three is the action of three Three-fold Flames. The I AM Presence, the Christ Self and the Three-fold Flame in the heart make an action of the Three times Three, three Three-fold Flames. The I AM Presence of each of the Twin Rays and the God-Flame from Whom They sprang make another action of the Power of the Three times Three.

Coupling action with knowledge and understanding produces *works;* Incorporating instruction into action (co-operating with action) gets results, which is what has been required through the ages.

"To know, to dare, to do and be silent" is the phrase given to the outer world; the inner Law is, be silent and dare to do that which you know.

Now that the cleaning up process or at least the drastic actions are pretty well taken care of, we enter into another phase of action, a somewhat different procedure and line of application.

The hope is that the reader can accept and utilize this information and instruction; make contact with his own I AM Presence and the Divine Beings, thereby become an asset to the Hierarchy, the planet and this scheme of creation.

Know your own Christ Self *is* the understanding Presence within you.

*   *   *

Further explanation in regard to the seven bodies as given on page 408, was given by beloved Kwan Yin in February 1954.

The "fall of man", incapacitated the conscious mind to function and to bring back the remembrance of the activities in higher Spheres and for the most part made inaccessible the conscious use of the Christ Self, the Causal and Electronic Bodies of the people. The four lower bodies were drawn down by the senses into the sub-strata of the etheric plane, and even they do not function in their natural spiritual habitat.

The conscious mind should be able to function in each Sphere and draw back the gifts and activities of It into the world of form.

The Electronic Presence and the Three-fold Flame should function in the First Realm. The Causal Body was destined to function in the Second Realm. The Christ Self originally functioned in the Third Sphere, and the etheric body, which functions now mostly in the psychic and astral realm; originally held the Divine pattern in the Fourth Sphere, where the Christ Selves presently abide. The mental body functioned in the Fifth Sphere. It was the activity of drawing the services of the inner Realms into form. The emotional body was to function in the Sixth Sphere, and its service was to pour forth the nature of the Godhead. The physical body was to function in the Seventh Sphere.

That is why beloved Master Saint Germain began through the contact of the outer consciousness, through the physical body, in the Seventh Sphere to help that consciousness work its way back into the heart of God, as it was originally.

INDEX

A

a

B

C

D

E

Earth, 206 to 208, 211 to 220, 226, 228, 229, 231, 232, 234, 235, 242, 243, 245, 249, 252, 253, 267, 272, 279, 282, 290, 299, 305 to 307, 311 to 313, 321, 326, 338, 240, 247, 366, 382, 385, 391, 393, 394, 403, 404, 409 to 420, 441, 445; Center of, 339

East, 313, 385, 411, 442

Education, 274, 333, 385, 388, 422, 442; Educator, 313

Effect, 230, 233, 252

Effort, 243, 251, 262, 321, 427

Egypt, 235, 238, 239, 257, 268, 275, 278, 344, 345, 428

Electricity, 399, 443

Element, 299, 338 to 341, 396, 401, 403

Elemental, 205, 208, 211, 216 to 218, 220 to 224, 239, 241, 254, 275, 277, 286, 293, 295, 315, 323 to 325, 327, 338, 340, 341, 342, 369, 378, 379, 381, 395, 416, 421, 422, 445; Body, 215; Life, 229, 343, 394; Gnome, 338; Salamander, 300; Sylph, 341; Undine, 340

Elixir, 234, 257, 258, 262, 349, 420, 436

Elohim, 205, 206, 212, 239, 292 to 298, 305, 343, 381, 385, 387, 399, 400, 407, 414, 415, 417, 451; of Peace, 297, 391; of Purity, 294, 295, 407

Embodiment, 210, 211, 213, 214, 215, 219 to 222, 231, 234, 236, 238, 246, 255, 256, 258 to 261, 265, 267, 272, 273, 275 to 278, 281, 282, 285, 286, 287, 290, 306, 310, 311, 313, 317, 318, 325, 330, 339, 341 to 343, 347 to 349, 353, 356 to 358, 363, 366, 369, 379, 394, 419; in between, 308, 413, 425

Embody, 63, 141, 209, 210, 216, 219, 229, 255, 302, 308, 315, 321, 362

Emotional, 322, 331, 340, 387, 411; World, 49, 378

Enlightenment, 254, 271, 311, 333, 388, 440; Enlightened One, 309

Entity, 217, 224, 244, 351

Eriel, 357, 358, 368, 369, 444

Etheric, 207, 211, 214, 215, 230, 387, 411; City, 237, 266, 305, 336, 348, 405, 413, 414; Realm, 231, 232, 292, 301, 366, 410, 413, 416, 420, 425, 427, 432, 436 to 438, 444, 445, 448; Record, 227, 230, 244, 258, 282, 303, 415, 416

Etherealize, 212, 390, 392, 393, 438

Example, 255, 267, 309, 438

Eye, All-seeing, 230, 296, 396, 415; Eyes, Book I, 96, 107, 111 to 113, 115

F

Faculties, 212, 215, 235, 293, 396, 438

Faith, 279, 281, 288, 388, 391, 433, 444, 445; Being, 286, 287, 289, 398, 399

G

R

S